A Guide for Building Trust Among Neighbors, Developers,
Planning Officials and Environmental

SMARTER LAND-USE
PROJECT MODELING KIT

# *Collaborative*
# Land Use Planning

## Karl Kehde

Printed in the United States of America

May 2007

Fourth Edition

ISBN 0-9705069-0-2


Published by
LUFNET (Land Use Forum Network, Inc.)
*a 501c3 non-profit organization*
208 Courthouse Drive
Morrisville, NC 27560


For additional copies of *Collaborative Land Use Planning*
or the *Collaborative Planning Kit,*
please contact the publisher or
visit the website: www.landuse.org

Your questions and comments are welcome.
You may contact Karl Kehde at
karl@landuse.org

# ACKNOWLEDGMENTS

The Smarter Land Use Project has been a broad-based team effort for more than twelve years. The people whose personal quotes you will read throughout the book were each active in dozens of meetings on specific proposed projects. The individuals and foundations that supported this work financially over the twelve years are listed on page 146. Without their financial support this research would not have been possible. Many people in each of the roles have contributed to this work. You will read in Chapter Eight more about the specific contributions of many of these people. Just a few of the key people are acknowledged here.

**Planning board members:** Julie Allen, Joyce Copleman, Tony Garrett, Mary Ellen Lister, Tom McPeek.

**Elected town officials:** Ted Chase, Donna Griff, Hope Lamb, Ruth Smith.

**Environmentalists:** Candy Ashmun, Beryl Doyle, Mannajo Greene, Miriam MacGillis, Philip Marden, Margaret McGarrity, David Moore, Norman Owen, Evonn Reiersen, Carolyn Vidala.

**Neighborhood leaders:** Andrea Bergman, Joan Duckloe, Gogo Ferguson, Karen Fritz, Susan Hirshberg, Joel McGreen, Saralyn Myers, Phyllis and Paul Smith.

**Developers:** John deNeufville, Scott Dignes, Michael Laino, Jim Rouse.

**Attorneys:** William Cox, Brad Day, Marvin Fish, Francis Gavin, Kevin Kelly, Paul Nussbaum, Joel Russell.

**Realtors:** Robert Becker, Jean Burgdorff, Davis Chant, Gerry Manger, Jean Roveda, Peg Ungerlieder.

**Landowners:** Leonard Hill, Laura Kane, Bill Leavens, Jack Smith.

**Planners:** Dianne Brake, Cynthia Hill, Judy Hnat, Peter Meyer, Eric Snyder.

**Government officials:** Wes Henry, Richard Binetsky.

I also very much appreciate the continuous support and understanding over the years of this project from Michael Giuliano, Ruth Beebe Hill, Brendan Kehde, Cynthia Koenig, and Donna Ryburn.

The preparation of this book has been a remarkably faithful team effort. Jim Fingar greatly facilitated presentation of the ideas with his extraordinary editing. A patient listener and brilliant organizer, he helped clarify the lessons learned by the Smarter Land Use Project and made sure that the book's organization and words communicated those lessons. Mark Hughes communicates in a few strokes ideas that were very hard to put into words. His illustrations demonstrate his wonderful perception and humor, and are a great addition to the book and to the Project. Sue Ball produced an attractive and compelling layout for this guidebook by dealing beautifully with a myriad of success stories, images, and quotations – and then assembling the book. Beth Berry did the copyediting on a hectic schedule laden with revisions, with a dogged attention to detail. David Emmerling contributed the directing, filming, and editing of the CD.

# TABLE OF CONTENTS

**INTRODUCTION**

# TABLE OF CONTENTS

# TABLE OF CONTENTS

## CHAPTER EIGHT
### History of the Smarter Land Use Project ......... 143

## APPENDIX
### Forms You Can Use ................................ 157

## Introduction

As a community we make many efforts to encourage the kind of friendly vitality we all want in our neighborhoods. We form clubs, build parks, and manage sports teams. We enjoy community celebrations of holidays. We have both government and volunteer efforts to promote justice and fight poverty. We have anti-litter campaigns. Lessons are taught in homes, schools, and at religious services. We spend money for law enforcement, neighborhood schools, branch libraries, and light pole banners promoting community activities. We make all those efforts and many more. Why aren't we doing better? Why do we have deteriorating inner city neighborhoods and compartmentalized Sprawl in the suburbs? What could we be doing better?

From the research I realized that enhancing the sense of community in our settlements is very difficult to achieve with a land development design and approval process that assumes that the agendas of developers, environmentalists, neighbors of proposed projects, and planning boards are likely to be in conflict. The regulations for our land development design and approvals actually assume conflict and are written to protect the rights of parties in dispute. Protecting rights is important in the event that a dispute erupts, but that can't be the guiding principle for land use planning. In order to build a community-enhancing project on the ground, a community-enhancing (collaborative) process is required to create it. In fact, at the same time the land use decision system is protecting people's rights in cases of disputes, the system needs to allow and encourage cooperation. Complying with regulations that protect rights must not squelch productive, cooperative efforts. Unfortunately, that is what is happening now. Cooperative, creative planning for our communities is inhibited by the current system. How do we get from where we are to where we need to be?

It is difficult to enhance community spirit, when the land use decision makers are in conflict.

# INTRODUCTION

To answer that question we need to highlight another lesson learned: good structures alone do not make a good community.

There are places and structures that contribute to the vitality of a community. There are places you have been where people naturally relax, smile, and get along with each other. What are they? Parks, pedestrian malls, gardens, playgrounds, libraries, and cafes. There are also structures that make some people feel safer and happier. A secure bikeway/walkway from school to home, or from home to the library or playground, is often mentioned. People feel better about their neighborhood if children can get around it safely. Beautiful vistas and public art can have a beneficial effect on community life. We need more of these positive places, and each neighborhood presents particular opportunities for such structures, but something else is needed as well. What?

Imagine for a moment two groups of people that don't like each other. Sadly it is easy to think of many such feuding groups from around the world. Now imagine those groups transplanted into the most beautiful, efficient, and well designed neighborhood you can imagine. Will the beautiful physical environment last?

A neighborhood needs to be maintained, and it requires tender, loving care. To improve or maintain the physical structure of a neighborhood requires good community relations. That serenity will endow them with energy to invest in their neighborhood. In fact, the beauty and harmony of the structures on the ground will become a reflection of the quality of the relationships among the inhabitants of the area. What you have on the ground in your community is a reflection of the quality of the community life that exists there. What are the factors that improve the quality of community life?

> **Good physical structure alone does not make a happy community.**

> **To improve or maintain the physical structure of a neighborhood requires good community relations.**

> "With this process the planning board has the opportunity to be a part of plans that actually reflect their town, rather than dealing with a concept brought in by an almost alien intruder. So, I think planning board members could really be working on something that they would enjoy. What an opportunity for them!"
>
> *Peter Meyer, President, Professional Planning and Engineering, Cedar Knolls, NJ*

Flexibility, creativity, and teamwork are needed to tend to the structure of the community . . .

There are many ways that community life is improved. The Smarter Land Use Project has found that, when it comes to planning development projects, the factors needed to improve the quality of community life are flexibility, creativity, and teamwork. Each land development project is done at a specific time and in a specific place, each of which has certain human and physical needs and potential. No master plan and no amount of land development regulation can address the problems and opportunities that surround each proposed development. The proposed project must be designed to deal with these problems and opportunities in a way that is unique to the project's time and place. Merely complying with zoning ordinances, designed to protect people's rights, limits the creativity of people involved in the planning process. Today, the developers take the lead in project planning and must focus on making a profit while obeying the ordinances. Their goals and skills don't equip them to focus on creatively studying the situation in order to make the best projects possible for the community. Any developer needs help from others to do that. The problem is that the flexibility, creativity, and teamwork needed for the best results can be severely inhibited by assuming disputes will erupt. Disputes do not have to erupt. There is a solution.

. . . and we can have them without changing the ordinances!

The solution doesn't require changes in the ordinances. It doesn't change the basic administration of land development. Yet, it allows creative, flexible visioning by neighbors, developer, planner, and environmentalists working collaboratively as one team. The project planning process is no longer restricted to considering regulated facilities that generate a profit for the developer in a project designed to be upheld in court should litigation be required.

The solution is a collaborative process that flourishes by designing projects expressly to include facilities that enhance community life – the interactions between neighbors. Projects that are primarily beautiful structures don't necessarily include facilities that enhance interactions between neighbors. Many people feel isolated and afraid inside nice homes. When the neighborhood includes features that enhance its sense of community, relationships improve among the residents and the community becomes safer, more beautiful, and a nicer place to live. Every proposed project offers the opportunity to add some things to enhance community life at the same time the developer makes a profit. Our research has shown how that can happen.

Neighbors, developer, city planner, and environmentalists can create projects that enhance community life when they work as one team. We have also found that they can mold themselves into a strong team even if they begin from a state of distrust and hostility. It also turned out that community life and relationships are enhanced by the process itself, never mind the results of the process. That is great news! We have to go through the project design and refinement process anyway, and now there is a way that the process can, itself, become an engine for improving human relations and consequently producing a better community on the ground. And if that isn't enough good news – the planning board meetings become more pleasant and efficient – shorter meetings, less frustration, better results!

> When the neighborhood includes features that enhance its sense of community, relationships improve among the residents and the community becomes safer.

> A team-building design process yields a community-building project.

> "We're dealing with plans that have community support and not just planning board support, because the people in the community participated in the creation of those plans. And community support is terribly important to us."
> **Ted Chase, Planning Board Chairman and Town Council, Lewisboro, NY**

## CHAPTER ONE

# Collaborative Planning: Who? What? Why? How?

## Contents

# Collaborative Planning: Who? What? Why? How?

*If you selected a shirt to wear the same way we select a land development to build, you would let the shirt manufacturer make your selection based on shirt regulations. That process alone is not likely to achieve "Smart Dressing." See page 16 for the solution.*

## Success — Byram, New Jersey
*Conflict resolved between neighbors and planning board over traffic from proposed project.*
*Solution: Relationships improved. Roads narrowed. Density reduced. Walkways and park added.*

*In Byram the collaborative planning team revised a conventional twelve lot subdivision to include a walkway that made a loop through the project connecting two adjacent neighborhoods. They also created a totlot park near a small hemlock grove and rock outcrop that was to be blasted away for the new road. They recommended that the new road be narrower and follow the existing contours of the land so that the hemlock grove would be spared and become part of the park.*

"They had been battling for almost two years. There was a developer, two sets of neighbors and the planning board. Everybody was pretty frustrated. When we started the collaboration, no one was really talking to each other or knowing what to do. The big issue was that no one was talking to anybody! I mean feelings were that hurt! The planning board was in the hot seat.

"We said, 'Well, it's our community; what if we do it this way!' We met at one of the neighbors' houses with neighbors from both sides of the development and the developer. In six months it was resolved! We relocated buildings and put in lots of walking paths and green space. It's going to enhance the whole community; it's going to be a really pretty development, and it's going to work!"

**Audrey O'Connell, Collaborative Planning team**

"We had been locked in a difficult, disjointed situation with a lot of misunderstanding and no spirit of cooperation. With this process we found ourselves sitting in someone's dining room discussing the issues calmly. It was a whole other ballpark! In a private setting with a relaxed atmosphere, they can see who you are, you see who your neighbors are, and you address each other's concerns. It's much easier and much more fruitful. You

get a better understanding between neighbor and developer. No question about it!

"Now we are on excellent terms! I think it's really excellent. There is faith and trust on both sides. The greatest thing is when you sit down with the neighbors you get a feeling about those people who will be participating in the public meeting. For us, we actually saved some money because of what they wanted to see developed there. We don't have to do the wider roads mandated by the municipality. We have smaller roads and a little park and sidewalks. They came up with some good suggestions that are saleable items. So, we learned a lot, and we benefited."

**Dennis McConnell, Developer and Attorney**

The best thing about this collaborative planning is that it asked us to play a real role in the development of our community. We shared the table and spoke freely with the developer and local officials. We now can make ourselves a powerful part of the conceptualization process at the very start, when we have a real chance to help design good development. People share very similar ideas about what a community should be. This was our best chance to achieve it — and we did!"

**Margaret McGarrity, Environmental Commission**

# Who benefits from Collabortive Land Use Planning?

**NEIGHBOR**

### Neighbor

Are you a neighbor of a proposed land development who is concerned about the effect the proposed project will have on the quality of your life and your property values? If so, this book shows you how a proposed project is an opportunity for you to make your neighborhood *better*.

**DEVELOPER**

### Developer

Are you a developer proposing a project in a settled area who is concerned about an expensive and protracted permitting process that may wind up in the courts? Then this book is for you. It teaches a way to use your development expertise to work with local residents and environmental experts so that your project steadily improves and consistently gains public support throughout an efficient and even enjoyable approval process.

**ENVIRONMENTALIST**

### Environmentalist

Are you an environmentalist who is dismayed by Sprawl and the damage it is causing to the environment? Collaborative Land Use Planning gives you a way to insure that your voice can be heard and shows how a proposed development is a way to solve existing environmental problems.

**PLANNING COMMISSION MEMBER**

### Planning Commission Member

Are you a planning commission member or elected official who wishes that your work would achieve more productive improvement of your community with shorter, less controversial meetings? This book provides a technique for unifying the energy and expertise of neighbors, developers, and environmentalists to help you efficiently generate truly beneficial projects.

## Planner

Are you a planner who would like to help create projects that incorporate the best ideas for community improvement? This book gives you a process you can use to achieve stakeholder agreement on profitable projects that truly enhance the community.

**PLANNER**

## Realtor

Are you a realtor who avoids developable properties because closings can be complex, risky, and time-consuming? By using collaborative planning, you can smoothly get to closing on tough development projects while forging new friendships and improving land values.

**REALTOR**

## Attorney

Are you an attorney who wishes that land development did not have to be an adversarial proceeding? This book shows you a process for settling litigation that not only satisfies the litigants but actually improves the proposed project for the community.

**ATTORNEY**

## Business Person

Are you a business person who wants to build a new headquarters building or manufacturing plant? This book shows you a process you can use to work together with the community and build good will as you get your permits.

**BUSINESS PERSON**

*The illustrations in this guidebook are not intended to stereotype any profession.*

> "I really benefited from partaking in collaborative planning by being involved with citizens that care. It enabled us to work in a positive emotional environment. It's a positive way to be creative in engineering and planning."
>
> *Peter Meyer, President, Professional Planning and Engineering, Cedar Knolls, NJ*

Every proposed land
development
is an opportunity to
improve its
surrounding
neighborhood.

## Why Read This Book?

This book is a practical guide to help you build a better place to live.

We all want to live in nice communities that become better and better with every new "development," yet many people are dissatisfied with the way their communities are evolving. During 12 years of meetings with boards, neighborhood groups, developers, and environmental groups, the Smarter Land Use Project discovered a new way of thinking about land development. In the end, the Project devised a collaborative planning process that results in smarter land use.

The rest of this chapter will give you background information on the collaborative approach. Chapters Two through Seven and the Appendix give you a practical guide so that you can initiate and benefit from a collaborative land use planning process, regardless of your role or experience. Chapter Eight tells the history of the Smarter Land Use Project.

## What Is Smarter Land Use?

Smarter land use adds
community-enhancing
projects to existing
settled areas.

Smarter land use results when land development is specifically designed to benefit its adjacent human and wildlife communities.

We all live on land that has been developed. Humans change the environment that nature provides in an effort to have more comfort, security, and beauty. Our ancestors built houses, farms, trails, and workplaces. Our towns are enriched by libraries, theaters, playgrounds, and meeting places. We are ready for an effective way to improve our environment and enhance our sense of community as we continue to create habitat for our increasing population and our changing needs.

A collaborative planning process that integrates proposed projects into their existing neighborhoods has emerged after years of experimentation. This process doesn't change the current legal and administrative structures that control land development. Rather, it adds a voluntary but powerful technique that helps the existing administrative procedures work more smoothly and productively. Arguing and lawsuits decrease, and projects and their surrounding neighborhoods improve. This collaborative process achieves smarter land use and enables Smart Growth.

> Collaborative planning is an effective way to include community-enhancing features in every project.

## Smart Growth vs. Sprawl

Recently the public's concern about the problems caused by land development has been deepening. The terms Sprawl and Smart Growth are now widely used to help us think about these issues. Urban decay makes people flee to the suburbs. Unfortunately, the same land development process which caused urban decay has been used to develop suburban areas. Sprawl has been the result.

Although it is clearly understood that there are problems associated with Sprawl, it is still the most common type of new land development. These projects intensify traffic, environmental, and social problems to the point where people want to escape, creating a demand for new land development in less densely populated areas and perpetuating the Sprawl cycle.

*Sprawl adds to environmental, traffic, and social problems.*

> "Residents had been looking to reestablish their roots, so when they say, 'I'm FROM someplace,' it's a place people will recognize and say, 'Oh, yes, that's a lovely place to be from.' "
> **Ted Chase, Planning Board Chairman, Lewisboro, NY**

**End Sprawl with projects designed expressly to enhance existing neighborhoods.**

To break the cycle, many communities are seeking to adopt laws to minimize the spread of Sprawl. Unfortunately, laws haven't worked well for this. Rather than make more laws, an alternate strategy is to end the demand for Sprawl, thereby making it obsolete. The way to end the demand for Sprawl is to improve the quality of life in settled areas so that people do not wish to flee to less settled areas. Edge, in-fill, and revitalization development in existing neighborhoods can be planned expressly to accomplish this task. The collaborative planning process, explained in the following chapters, makes this possible.

Smarter land development or redevelopment is designed specifically to benefit its adjacent human and wildlife community. It builds community spirit, solves existing problems, and further develops the best character and identity of the area. It increases property values and reduces the expense of community services. Smarter land development is supported by both residents and developers and is easily approved through existing administrative channels.

**Smart Growth is achieved one project at a time.**

Smarter land development is how Smart Growth is achieved – one project at a time.

*The current approved process focuses on minimizing damage rather than maximizing enhancement.*

## Summary of the Current Land Development Process

Developers use their resources to acquire land and "develop" it to make a profit. Often a project provides a profit for the developer but causes problems for the adjacent community.

In response, towns adopt development regulations to protect the interests of their citizens. The regulations generally focus on minimizing the damage caused by development. They do this by regulating the permitted types of land use (residential, commercial, industrial) and by limiting the amount of negative impact development can have on noise, traffic, scenery, natural and historic resources, etc. Each stakeholder (developer, citizens, environmentalists) fights for adoption of regulations that help protect their own special interests.

Each political jurisdiction (borough, town, township, city, etc.) has a planning commission or board that is appointed by elected officials. Responsibilities of the planning commission include overseeing and coordinating development, reviewing proposed land development projects to ensure they comply with development regulations, and then approving the plans for construction if they comply. Another responsibility of the planning commission is to recommend improvements to the development regulations (or ordinances) to the elected officials, who then vote to adopt them.

Communities that have development regulations usually have divided the town into development zones (residential, commercial, industrial, etc.). Each zone has different requirements for lot size, building use and height, parking spaces, road width, etc. Some political jurisdictions also appoint a zoning board of adjustment which can review certain projects that do not comply with the development regulations. This board has the authority to permit certain variances to the regulations and to approve projects for construction even if they do not comply with the regulations. Zoning boards provide a degree of flexibility to development regulations. Such flexibility is needed, but the current system is often the source of very contentious debate.

Building uses and heights, parking, lot sizes, set backs, and buffers can be regulated by ordinances . . .

. . . but how do we get public greens, connecting walkways, recreational facilities, diversified housing, and other community-enhancing features?

"What greater reassurance can the planning board have that this is the right thing than have the citizens of their town and the neighbors of this particular project and the owner of the land or the person that's going to ultimately develop it come to them together and say, 'This is what we would like to see on this land!' "

*Peter Meyer, President, Professional Planning and Engineering, Cedar Knolls, NJ*

The developer must create a plan that complies with the regulations or obtain necessary variances. The project also must be profitable for the developer to build. The developer usually acquires the property, creates the development plan, presents the plan for approval, and then builds the project. In some situations the developer is the landowner. In such cases, once development plans for the property are approved, they may be sold with the property to a builder.

The developer must create a plan that complies with the regulations and is profitable to build.

*Today's developer*

Today, the neighbors are notified after the developer has created the plan.

After the developer discusses the proposed plan with the planning commission, the plan must be presented to the neighbors by the developer in a public hearing. If the neighbors do not like some aspect of the developer's plan, they have no legal right to force a change in the plan if the plan complies with the regulations. There is usually little or no focus on community-enhancing features.

If the requested changes reduce the developer's profit and are not required for the plan to comply with the regulations, the developer does not have to make the changes. This can be frustrating for the neighbors, planning board, and developer. The response of the board is most often to suggest to the neighbors that they help upgrade the regulations so that it doesn't happen the _next_ time. There is nothing they can do about it _this_ time.

THE CURRENT PROCESS CAN BE FRUSTRATING FOR EVERYONE!

Environmental commissions are usually appointed by elected officials. Their responsibilities may include creating a natural resources inventory for the town and suggesting regulations that protect the environment from unnecessarily destructive land development. They also may review the developer's proposed plans and suggest changes that protect water quality and other natural features.

The planning commission, developer, environmental commission, and neighbors use attorneys, planners, and engineers as necessary to provide expertise in interpreting the development regulations and defending their particular rights. Each participant in the project planning and approval process takes on a role – wears a specific hat – as the drama unfolds.

"The focus is on a subject that people are very, very much concerned about and care so terribly much about, and just allow them to work together. I'm talking about the developers and local residents and local officials. Just get them together and let them focus on the short term and long term needs and the common solutions to those needs."

_Ted Chase, Planning Board Chairman, Lewisboro, NY_

Usually planning commissions, zoning boards, and environmental commissions are comprised of citizens who serve without compensation. Developers, planners, attorneys, engineers, and realtors generally earn their living from land development work.

Planning commissions, zoning boards, and environmental commissions usually serve without compensation.

PLANNING COMMISSIONS    ZONING BOARDS    ENVIRONMENTAL COMMISSIONS

UNSUNG HEROES

The roles played by these individuals and boards may differ slightly from state to state. Detailed information can be found in the municipal or state regulations or from a local land-use attorney.

## A New Paradigm for Land Development

Development plans must comply with the regulations and receive approval from the planning board before the developer can build the project. Thus, each project is planned by the developer to comply with the regulations while earning a satisfactory profit.

The current planning and approval system is based on a paradigm (set of assumptions) in which land development is expected to have at least some negative impact on the quality of life. This paradigm generates the vigilance which can set environmental groups and neighbors of proposed projects against the developer. Despite the regulations and the hard work of the planning board, which is often caught in the middle, the resulting project is often a compromise, impacting negatively on the surrounding community and including few community-enhancing features. Research by the Smarter Land Use Project over the last twelve years discovered that some assumptions of this paradigm are not true and these false assumptions yield confrontation and Sprawl.

> Sprawl occurs because today's paradigm assumes development to have negative impact.

*Mistaken assumptions are yielding confrontation and Sprawl.*

The research shows that a different paradigm is actually true. A land development procedure in accordance with the new paradigm will yield community-enhancing land development, end Sprawl, and achieve Smart Growth. By improving the assumptions that guide our thinking about land development, we shift the paradigm.

> "Coming out of this I would expect would be a better sense of community, a better sense of town, a better sense of wholeness."
> **Peter Meyer, President, Professional Planning and Engineering, Cedar Knolls, NJ**

Let's compare the assumptions of the current paradigm with the improved assumptions of the new paradigm.

## Better assumptions allow better solutions

A truer paradigm yields community-enhancing land development. The developer can become a hero.

### Current Land Development Paradigm

Proposed development is likely to have negative impact on the surrounding neighborhood.

Developer's goal is to maximize profit while complying with regulations. Neighbors are vigilant that the project *minimizes damage* to their quality of life.

The developer frequently wants more development, while the neighbors want less development with bigger buffers and setbacks.

Environmentalists want to stop the project or change it to *maintain* environmental quality.

Focus is *inward* on the project itself to insure that it complies with regulations and minimizes damage to the environment and adjacent neighborhoods.

Development is governed by master plan, regulations, and the permitting process.

### New Land Development Paradigm

Proposed development is an opportunity to make the surrounding neighborhood better.

Developer will make a good profit building a project that *maximizes enhancement* to the quality of life in the surrounding neighborhood.

Developer's expertise and neighbors' awareness of neighborhood conditions together can create the project of greatest value to the neighborhood.

Environmentalists and developer can work together to configure the project to solve environmental problems and *enhance* the environment.

Focus is *outward* on the surrounding neighborhood and how the project can maximally enhance the quality of life and the environment.

Development is governed by master plan, regulations, voluntary creative collaboration, and the permitting process.

Smart Growth occurs when the paradigm for land development shifts to the expectation that each proposed project in a settled area will be designed expressly to *benefit* the surrounding neighborhood. How can development enhance life in the surrounding neighborhood? This becomes the new focus for development. Voluntary, creative collaboration will find ways to do this *and* allow the developer to make a good profit. The developer, neighbors, city planner, and environmentalists can support the neighborhood-enhancing agenda and work as a team to conceptalize the project. The larger agenda also allows them to achieve their special-interest goals.

> Smart Growth occurs when the paradigm shifts to the expectation of enhancement.

*Enhancing life in the surrounding neighborhood becomes the new focus of land development plans.*

Just reading the table on the preceding page starts to shift your paradigm about land development. It doesn't hurt too much, does it? It doesn't hurt, but you might feel confused about what you should do now. The rest of this chapter provides additional mind-expanding ideas so that you will be ready for roll-up-your-sleeves, practical advice in Chapter Two.

Sprawl results from an incomplete project design process.

## Current Conceptualization Process Is Incomplete

The current land development conceptualization process often produces Sprawl instead of Smart Growth because the process is limited to these elements:

Development concept complies with regulations
Developer makes a profit

These elements are not enough. More issues must be considered when land development plans are conceived.

## Completing the Conceptualization Process

Here are the considerations that are missing from the current process:

- How can the project benefit neighborhood life?
- How can the project bring out the best in the community?
- What architecture expresses the best existing character?
- What configuration looks best on the landscape?
- What design features most help the environment?
- Which configuration most supports neighborhood values?
- Are the facilities sustainable? Will they last?

*Community-enhancing considerations complete the conceptualization process and yield "smart dressing."*

When project designers deal with these considerations, community-enhancing features dominate the plans they create.

Examples of community-enhancing features are public greens, recreational facilities, affordable housing, architecture in the best character of the existing neighborhood, wildlife sanctuaries, and walkways through the project from adjacent neighborhoods directly to important destinations. Many more are included on the Checklist of Community-Enhancing Features in the Appendix. These features foster a sense of community, increase safety and emotional support, help the aging population and children at risk, reduce traffic congestion, and enhance the natural environment, the surrounding neighborhood, and the project itself.

Community-enhancing features are generally not included in projects today because (1) there is no cooperative forum for a systematic evaluation of the surrounding neighborhood to see which features would be of greatest benefit, and (2) the approval process is confrontational, preoccupying the developer, the neighbors, and the boards with defending their agendas and building a basis for successful litigation.

## Four Principles of Collaborative Land Use Planning

How can project designers be encouraged to deal with these additional considerations and include the appropriate community-enhancing features? Since every project is located in a different place and helps a different neighborhood, zoning regulations cannot require these features or specify which ones to include. Our research discovered that the above questions will be consistently considered and the appropriate community-enhancing features will be included whenever the four principles of Inclusive Team-building, Outward Focus, Enhancement, and Sustainability are applied in planning a project. The following pages review each of these principles and how they are applied to land development conceptualization to consistently achieve smarter land use and ultimately Smart Growth.

Smart Growth projects include community-enhancing features such as public greens, connecting walkways, affordable housing, wildlife sanctuaries, and recreational facilities.

Community-enhancing features will be included in land development plans when four principles are applied.

"Collaborative planning improves the plan because it has input from three different areas as opposed to just coming from a developer's idea. And any plan that has more input, you know, it's got more profitability because it's more creative. So it's definitely improved."
*Audrey O'Connell, collaborative planning team, Environmental Commission, Byram, NJ*

### Principle #1: Inclusive Team-building

The goal of smarter land development is to add as much value and vitality to the surrounding neighborhood as possible. When the project designers understand the neighborhood surrounding the project, its assets, liabilities, problems, and potential, they know which community-enhancing features to include in the project.

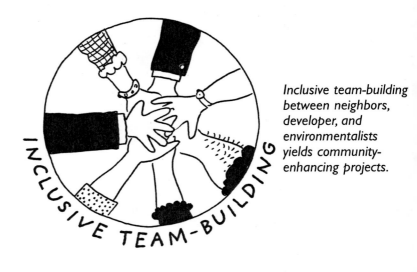

*Inclusive team-building between neighbors, developer, and environmentalists yields community-enhancing projects.*

When the design team includes expertise in construction, financing, marketing, and the environment, they can find ways to include the most community-enhancing features in the project. Voluntary, creative collaboration of neighbors, developer, city planner, environmentalists, and other interested citizens is the best forum for producing smarter land use. Our research shows that the more inclusive and unified the collaborative team, the more community-enhancing features will be included in the project.

Today, when the developer's pre-made plan is presented to the planning board, neighbors and environmentalists during the approval process, confrontation frequently results because they must review the plan from the perspective of minimizing damage to their specific interests. The damage control mentality polarizes the neighbors, the developer, and the environmentalists by placing each of them on the defensive. The defensive posture shuts down community-oriented thinking and results in a costly approval process and a compromised project with few, if any, community-enhancing features.

The community-enhancing features of smarter land use begin to appear when the neighbors, city planners, developers, and environmentalists start to work together. Inclusive teambuilding can work well in land development planning because the neighbors, developer, and environmentalists can each visualize and support an overall community-building agenda that includes their special interest agendas. Once collaboration begins, participants see that the more they cooperate and share their expertise, the better their opportunity for achieving their special interest agendas. The teamwork generates a wealth of creative synergy and clear, relaxed thinking that can result in projects that actually exceed individual special-interest agendas and yield significant community-enhancing features.

Inclusive team-building in achieving smarter land use means that neighbors, developer, city planner, and environmentalists work as a team to conceptualize the project. The collaborative planning process detailed in Chapter Two gives them the forum, the steps, and the tools for steadily improving their teamwork. Chapter Four provides specific collaboration aids that will help unify the neighbors, developer, and environmentalists concerned about a specific project, regardless of their history.

> **Defensiveness among the stakeholders shuts down creative thinking.**

> **Inclusive team-building works because the team's community-building agenda includes each member's special-interest agenda.**

> "It's a win-win situation for us because basically what we're trying to do is create an option for a better way to develop the land. We are not ruling out the conventional approach and, therefore, when you have an option, you're always better off."
>
> *John deNeufville, developer, Mendham, NJ*

## Principle #2: Outward Focus

Today, the focus of land development planning is inward on the project site and on planning the project to be profitable and comply with regulations. It is assumed that the land development regulations will protect quality of life and property values in the neighborhood surrounding the project. There is no requirement or procedure for specifically planning the project to include features that enhance the surrounding neighborhood. Surrounding neighborhoods are not shown on plans except for structures within 100 feet of the property line.

Projects that are planned with this inward focus tend to encourage isolation because they are not connected to adjacent projects with walkways, architecture, and other community-enhancing features. Since they are not planned expressly to solve social and environmental problems in the surrounding neighborhood, they usually increase automobile traffic and intensify the social and environmental problems, thereby adding to Sprawl.

For smarter land use to occur, collaborative project planning must use an "outward focus." Assets and liabilities of the surrounding neighborhood must be inventoried and evaluated so that the project can be planned expressly to benefit its surrounding area.

With an outward focus, neighbors, developer, and environmentalists evaluate social, environmental, and economic characteristics of the surrounding neighborhood to determine where there are opportunities for improvement. Then, as the project is configured, community-enhancing features are selected to solve existing problems and improve life as much as possible.

The proposed project site, when seen as the "center of the donut," becomes the key to knitting the surrounding neighborhood together. Walkways/bikeways can be planned on the site to directly connect important gathering places, such as churches, schools, post office, and shopping, to residents on opposite sides of the site. In addition to residences or commercial buildings, facilities such as public

**Existing problems are solved when project design focuses on enhancing the surrounding neighborhood.**

**The proposed project is an opportunity to knit together the surrounding neighborhood.**

greens, pavilions, recreational facilities, and benches can be planned along the connecting walkways as opportunities to bring people together. Architecture that best promotes the historic identity of the neighborhood can be used in the new buildings.

A project uplifts and brings out the best in the surrounding neighborhood when it focuses outward rather than inward. The project thus becomes the centerpiece of the surrounding area and gains higher value and appeal. By focusing outward and enhancing life in the surrounding neighborhood, the project achieves its greatest value.

**Chapter Two gives you the step-by-step collaborative planning process.**

*The proposed project becomes the heart of its surrounding neighborhood.*

"As a result of collaborative planning I got to know quite a few of the people who live bordering this property, and their honest input has been very useful to me. Secondly, to have a plan that is supported by quite a large number of the citizens surrounding the property, which is our goal, is something that's almost unheard of, and it takes what is usually the biggest problem in developing land and turns it into a benefit."
*John deNeufville, developer, Mendham, NJ*

### Principle #3: Enhancement

Today, land development projects are designed to comply with the regulations, and then approved to minimize damage to the area influenced by the project.

One problem with working toward the goal of minimizing damage is that it usually results in at least some damage. To get no damage the goal must be to maximize enhancement. Then there will usually be at least some enhancement.

A second problem of working toward a goal of protection or minimizing the damage is that somebody always gets defensive because they see themselves as the person or group being protected against. For example, efforts to minimize damage and protect the environment tend to polarize the neighbors, developer, town officials, and environmentalists because people become defensive. Damage-control mentality takes over. Collaboration, clear thinking, and creativity are hampered, and community-enhancing features are shelved.

> The word "protection" puts people on the defensive. "Enhancement" puts them on the same team.

Consider the effect of the word "Protection" in the name of the Environmental Protection Agency. It makes some people offenders and puts them on the defensive. That then puts the Environmental Protection Agency on the defensive. On the other hand, suppose the name were changed to the Environmental Enhancement Agency? Would that take the offenders off the defensive and encourage them to invest in enhancing the environment as much as possible? With the *support* of the Environmental Enhancement Agency? I think so. When the assumption is enhancement, every project becomes an opportunity to make the community a better place to live. Then, land development actually develops the community's land into a better and better place.

*When the assumption is enhancement, every project becomes an opportunity to make its neighborhood a better place to live.*

Each land development project can be planned expressly to include community-enhancing features. Money for community-enhancing features is available from philanthropic sources when (1) a clear vision of placement, use, and benefits of such features can be presented, and (2) there is a clear consensus and enthusiasm from neighbors, developer, environmentalists, and town officials that such features are desired. The collaborative planning team described in Chapter Two achieves these two objectives. Smarter land use results in community enhancement instead of damage control.

## Principle #4: Sustainability

Sustainability is achieved when land development uses renewable resources and does not cause undue drain on non-renewable resources. In order to achieve sustainability in a land development project, the process for designing the project must also be sustainable. A confrontational planning and approval process is not sustainable because it drains the energy of the boards, developers, planners,

"In my view it's best for the collaborative planning team to do it themselves as much as possible, to let all of the good things that people have to offer just flow to the surface, and to provide that kind of a process."
**Ted Chase, Planning Board Chairman, Lewisboro, NY**

neighbors, and environmentalists. In fact, sustainability issues are seldom discussed in planning board meetings because people are busy defending their agendas and are focused primarily on density, buffers, and setbacks.

In our research we found that when the neighbors, developer, planners, and environmentalists work as a team so that they can include community-enhancing features in the project, they would readily discuss the development configuration in terms of energy and resource conservation and the use of renewable resources.

> A confrontational process is a non-sustainable drain on problem-solving resources, and the project is likely to reflect that drain.

*Collaboration adds resources.*

*Confrontation drains resources.*

Smarter land use reflects a smarter project design and approval process. Selected locations for the facilities, as well as the construction, maintenance, and use of the facilities, have long-term benefits and do not drain non-renewable resources. The sustainability of a proposed development pattern is considered in terms of how it achieves social and community health, economic security, environmental enhancement, application of intellectual resources, and spiritual and moral goals.

## How to Apply the Four Principles

Application of the principles of inclusive team-building, outward focus, enhancement, and sustainability is assured by following the collaborative planning process described in Chapter Two. It is an easy, step-by-step process that any community can use on any size project.

Why collaborative planning? Because the project is not limited by lot boundaries. Improvement of the entire area influenced by the project is the goal.

Neighbors, developers, planners, and environmentalists who have followed the collaborative planning process have made the shift from defending role-based agendas to working as a team. The team seizes the opportunity presented by the proposed project to creatively and cooperatively make the surrounding neighborhood and the project a better place to live and work. The next chapter will lead you through this exciting process.

Smarter land use reflects a smarter project design and approval process.

"The discussion of the possibilities and the moving around of little models acts as a cross-fertilization of ideas about how an ultimate goal could be accomplished, and that's a good thing. That's what I found to be very beneficial."
*Paul Nussbaum, Attorney, Planning Board, and collaborative planning team, Hope, NJ*

# The Collaborative Planning Process

## Better projects and better neighborhoods through creative cooperation

## Contents

# The Collaborative Planning Process

## Better projects and better neighborhoods through creative cooperation

*"Being a part of their community, not just today but in terms of making a contribution to it in the long run, is something that is basically very meaningful to people, and given the opportunity to do it, they'll put up with a lot if they believe that they really can make that kind of a contribution."*

Ted Chase, Planning Board Chairman, Lewisboro, NY

## Success — Nanuet, New York
### Conflict: Commercial use in a residential area.
### Solution: Relationships improved. Buildings moved.

*In Nanuet a nursing home was proposed next to a residential neighborhood. The collaborative planning team relocated the proposed buildings to preserve a beautiful, mature woodland. A park was created with a rebuilt stream, pond, and walkways.*

"We had heard snippets of information that a major development was going to happen in our neighborhood, but nobody had any real information. There were very few details that we could actually get from the bureaucracy. There was a mysterious group that owned the property. There was smoke and nobody could see any fire. Somebody found this process on the internet and we called.

We used the collaborative planning process to first inform the neighbors that there was a different way to go about this, and that they could have a part. That started to build interest in actually participating and making a difference. Then we were able to use that to contact the developers and to show them that there is this other process that they can follow, and there are all these people interested in talking to them. And they actually came to a social discussion where we didn't talk about the development: a cookout with the neighbors at our house. It was wonderful; we had about 40 people here. They got to see we weren't a bunch of foot-stomping obstructionists; they found out who we are and what we like about this neighborhood. And we got to see that they weren't a bunch of greedy developers, and what it was that they were trying to accomplish. And, maybe most important, neighbors really got to know each other and reminisced about neighborhood events when they were growing up. It created a warm feeling for a lot of people. People that felt kind of isolated and alone, didn't feel so alone anymore. Then, in the group meetings we continued that and got first-hand information from the developer before it was too late to do anything about it.

When we went to the planning board, we had quite a few of people in the neighborhood engaged in the process. The aerial photo was a phenomenal piece of material to have at that meeting. The planning board said, "You have an aerial photo, let's put it up on the wall." From then on even the board members stood up and referred to the photo. The neighbors really understood how this project could be done in a way that would have a more positive effect on the community. Every single neighbor knew the facts, the most current information, so everyone was speaking clearly, concisely, intelligently, and calmly. So, very quickly the discussion came onto the ground that we were comfortable with. It was neighbors standing up and saying here are suggestions about how the development could be done so that it benefits the community, rather than gathering information or just saying 'no.' I think we were really heard. Buildings were changed and moved to preserve prime forest. Connecting walkways and serious landscaping were recommended by the board. We were very pleased.

From this process, I realized that not only is it important to be involved in shaping your community, but it is possible to really do that and to make a difference. I was surprised at how involved and civic-minded I actually could get. I was struck with the possibilities of this process to get people interested and really make this community into something. We had lived here six years, and in the few months of this process we met and got to know more neighbors than we had in the past six years. Now when we are gardening in the front yard, people drive by and say 'Hi, Jake.' It was terrific that we actually got to bring the neighborhood together and bring back a sense of community — even if nothing had changed on the development. This is a process that breaks down stereotypes and breaks through fears. It helps open up lines of communication and build trust. It is so much more efficient and everyone can feel good instead of some feeling like they lost!"

**Jake and Suzanne Lynn,
collaborative planning team leaders**

**Proposed development can be designed to improve your life.**

**See the Appendix for a Checklist of Community-Enhancing Features.**

## Introduction

*Is there a real estate project proposed near your neighborhood? Would you like to see this development improve your life and your property values? What community-enhancing features could be included in the project that would improve your life?*

Neighborhoods benefit from recreational facilities, public greens, affordable housing, wildlife sanctuaries, walkways that directly connect homes to important destinations, and other features that promote interaction and community spirit. Dozens of these features are listed in the Checklist of Community-Enhancing Features in the Appendix. How can these features be designed into the project that is proposed near your neighborhood?

*Neighbors invite the developer to join the collaborative planning team.*

"We met at one of the neighbor's houses and we had a group of neighbors from one side of the development and a group of neighbors from the other side of the development, and we had the developer."
**Audrey O'Connell, Environmental Commission, collaborative planning team, Byram, NJ**

The best way to design community-enhancing features into the proposed development is for its neighbors to invite the developer to join a collaborative planning team. The collaborative planning process depends on a team of people working together to achieve a level of creative problem solving that individuals alone can't achieve. The team includes interested neighbors of the proposed project, the developer, environmentalists, and other interested citizens who wish to devote their time to designing a community-enhancing project.

The neighbors host the collaborative planning process. They arrange meeting space and refreshments, get people to the meetings, and distribute the meeting agenda and other materials. This guidebook serves as a coach for the team – with tips to help beginners play well. No outside facilitator is needed. Meeting facilitator and note-taker roles are rotated among the participants. The team is self-owned and self-governed and may dissolve itself at any time.

Membership on a collaborative planning team is "inclusive," meaning that anyone who wants to participate is always welcome. Participation is voluntary. Participation in collaborative planning has no effect on the owner/developer's legal rights to use the property. The team gets the credit for designing the community-enhancing project, and shares with the planning board the credit for an efficient and enjoyable project permitting process.

**The neighbors host the collaboration.**

**No outside facilitator is needed. Facilitator and note-taker roles rotate among the participants. This guidebook serves as a coach – with tips to help beginners play well.**

**Regardless of past experience, neighbors, developer, and environmentalists usually want to work together.**

"It's a nice, informal way of getting people talking, getting people to take ownership of their town, of a development, of what they'd like to see in town, of their common space. And it reminds you to take care of your own land, to see its interdependence and how it affects your whole community."
*Audrey O'Connell, Environmental Commission, collaborative planning team, Byram, NJ*

Community-enhancing features upgrade the project and integrate it into the surrounding neighborhood.

Research done by the Smarter Land Use Project shows that, in addition to making new friends in the neighborhood, creative collaboration yields the best project plans and is relatively easy to initiate even when there is a history of confrontation between the interested parties. People usually prefer collaboration to conflict. All that is needed is a step-by-step process for the parties to follow. Collaborative planning allows a cohesive team to form for the sole purpose of integrating the proposed project into the surrounding neighborhood. This team designs the project to include community-enhancing features that upgrade the project and integrate it into the neighborhood. This guidebook is the coach of the collaborative planning team.

*The collaborative planning team with its coach.*

"Collaborative planning isn't always easy but it's worth doing because it works, because in the end it is worth it to have gone through it and come up with a better plan. It's a team building. We're in a community. We all live here. We all want to build a better community. Well, we need a process to work in the community to build that better community. And this process gives us that opportunity."
*Audrey O'Connell, Environmental Commission, collaborative planning team, Byram, NJ*

# How the Collaborative Planning Process Works:

## Step 1: Gather Materials

Every proposed project is an opportunity to improve its surrounding neighborhood. Three items will make this clear to the neighbors.

Give neighbors:
1. Map
2. Features Checklist
3. Invitation

**(1) A map that shows both the property to be developed and its surrounding neighborhood**

To create this map, borrow from the planning board a copy of the plan submitted by the developer. Then, get a local street map and outline the site of the project on the street map. Make copies of the portion of the street map that shows the outlined project site and the surrounding neighborhood. Include enough of the surrounding neighborhood to look like a donut around the project site, which is the hole in the donut.

*Make copies of a street map that shows the neighborhood as a donut around the project site.*

"I think one of the real advantages that came about, and it's an advantage to the whole community, is that everybody learned from this process. They learned about needs, they learned about themselves, they learned about the community, they learned about their neighbors, and they got to know each other."
**Ted Chase, Planning Board Chairman, Lewisboro, NY**

### (2) The Checklist of Community-Enhancing Features

Make copies of the Checklist of Community-Enhancing Features in the Appendix. Note: The Checklist has two sides. Be sure to copy both sides.

### (3) An invitation to a neighborhood meeting

Copy the Sample Invitation from the Appendix, fill in the blanks with the date, time, and place, and make as many copies as you need. A neighbor's house is probably the best place to meet. Otherwise, try another location in the neighborhood such as a church, school, library, or a community room in a local business.

## Step 2: Find interested neighbors of the proposed project

Distribute the invitations, your copies of the street map with the property outlined, and the Checklist of Community-Enhancing Features to the neighbors who live or work adjacent to the site of the proposed project.

It will help attendance at the neighborhood meeting if you distribute the invitations about a week before the meeting and then remind people with a phone call or a card the day before the meeting.

"When we had our first meeting, people were very uncomfortable to speak about planning. They felt that they knew nothing about it. But that's not true. We all live on land. We all have houses, we all have cars, we all live in community."

*Audrey O'Connell, Environmental Commission, collaborative planning team, Byram, NJ*

*Neighbors of the proposed project decide if they want to host the collaborative planning process.*

For each meeting, create, adopt, and follow a written meeting agenda based on the sample in the Appendix. At the first meeting, hand out copies of this chapter and review the seven steps and the Checklist of Community-Enhancing Features. See if some people would like to have another meeting and continue to the next step. Set the date for the next meeting and plan to invite more people. After every meeting, send the planning board a brief Update Letter *(see the sample in the Appendix)*.

> After every meeting, send an update letter to the planning board (see the sample in the Appendix).

## Step 3: Consider possible community-enhancing features to include in the project

Carefully review the Checklist of Community-Enhancing Features and check the features and facilities that might help life in the neighborhood surrounding the proposed project. Feel free to add your own ideas that could help in your particular location. In Step Five you will determine which features are practical to include in the project.

## Step 4: Meet with the developer

The developer knows how to build a project at a profit, and wants to build this project. The developer's expertise and desire to build this project are essential in designing

*The developer becomes a trusted member of the collaborative planning team.*

> "This process puts you in touch with the people in the community. So you're much more sensitized to what the community really needs and wants out of your land, and that, from just a marketing point of view, has to be useful input. Secondly, and probably more importantly, the citizens provided kind of a political base for the notion of doing things differently that the land owner himself couldn't possibly have generated without their support."
> **John deNeufville, Land Owner and Developer, Mendham, NJ**

community-enhancing features into the project in a way that is financially feasible for their construction. The developer becomes a trusted member of the collaborative planning team. Chapter Four explains how to build trust and friendship between the team members even when there has been previous confrontation. Invite the developer to all meetings after the first one or two neighborhood meetings. Discuss your ideas for community-enhancing features with the developer, and seek additional ideas.

## Step 5: Model the project to include community-enhancing features

Viewing the area from above is a great help in successfully integrating a proposed development into its surrounding neighborhood. An enlarged map or aerial photo of the project site and its "donut" is essential for the collaborative planning team to model the project. Chapter Five tells exactly how to obtain an aerial photo at the scale and size needed to model your project (from one acre to one hundred acres).

*Chapter Five tells how to get an enlarged aerial photo or map at the right size and scale for your project.*

*Viewing the site and its surrounding neighborhood from above helps in planning a better project.*

"Most of us had known each other slightly for years, but have never interacted with each other in such an in-depth way. We're creating an ongoing relationship amongst ourselves and I think we all enjoy that. And I think that propels a lot of people to keep coming, because they're enjoying it."

*Ruth Smith,*
*collaborative planning team,*
*Town Council, Planning*
*Board, Mendham, NJ*

Model the project directly on the map or aerial photo that shows the site and the surrounding neighborhood (the donut). Chapter Six explains the project modeling steps in detail and includes many tips. Briefly the procedure works this way: You will be using Post-It notes to mark important places. You will use yarn to experiment with possible locations for walkways, bikeways, and roads. You use the scale model buildings and recreational facilities cutouts from the Appendix or from the Collaborative Planning Kit to experiment with possible locations for those features.

**Model the project to include community-enhancing features directly on the map, or photo, of the project and its donut.**

*The project modeling sessions focus on increasing trust and making friends so that community-enhancing features may be more easily included.*

The model will continually improve as trust, friendship, and cooperation improve between the neighbors, developer, city planner and environmentalists. The Consensus Checklist in the Appendix provides guidelines for continually increasing trust. Copy it on the back of the meeting agenda. The project modeling sessions are primarily about improving trust and making friends, because when people make friends, they relax, become more creative, and get ideas that solve previously unsolvable problems. The community-enhancing features in the project ultimately reflect the trust, friendship, and community spirit that has been built between the interested parties.

"I've learned that it's possible to have strangers come together and meet in a creative, enthusiastic way over a long period of time to meet a common goal. I wouldn't have thought that this much enthusiasm would have been generated over this. So it makes me hopeful that there may be another way to develop land that goes beyond the conventional confrontation approach that has been used in the past."

*John deNeufville,*
*developer, Mendham, NJ*

Continue to hold collaborative planning meetings until the participants are satisfied that the project design includes the best possible community-enhancing features. Advertise the meetings and keep the planning board informed with the update letters.

## Step 6: Discuss the project with the planning board

The planning board usually likes the cooperation and the connectedness in project plans that result from the collaborative planning process. Make time to show them the collaboration and the project model as it is evolving. The board may have ideas for community-enhancing features as well as sources for funding their construction and maintenance. Show the project to the board by building it directly on the map or aerial photo of the surrounding neighborhood.

> The planning board usually likes the collaboration and the connectedness in the plans.

> "We were, I think, eight or nine at that first meeting. Then very quickly the group grew, almost doubled in size within the next couple of meetings and that's because the people that were there thought of other people that should be there, people that I hadn't thought to ask."
> **Ruth Smith, Collaborative planning team leader, town council, Mendham, NJ**

*Advertise the collaborative planning meetings.*

Sometimes approval of the most needed community-enhancing feature may require the planning board to grant a variance. When a model of the proposed project, including the community-enhancing feature, is presented to the planning board by the neighbors, developer, city planner, and environmentalists together, it is easy for the board to understand not only how the feature will benefit the surrounding neighborhood, but also that the neighbors, developer, city planner, and environmentalists are in agreement about the need for and the location of the feature.

**Present the project to the board by building it directly on the aerial photo that shows the surrounding neighborhood.**

*Neighbors and environmentalists make the presentation. The developer is present and in agreement.*

**Neighbors participate equally in the presentation, rather than one person doing the talking.**

Presentations to the planning board are best made by the neighbors and the environmentalists with the developer and city planner present to indicate their participation in the collaboration and their approval of the ideas presented. The presentation is most effective when as many neighbors as possible participate equally, rather than one person making the presentation. Each person shares their own thoughts about (1) the value of collaborative planning, (2) why they like a particular community-enhancing feature, and (3) how its location in the project was determined.

"In the planning board meetings themselves one of the things that you find is a very distinct difference just in terms of the appearance, where community residents are in fact coming forward with the developer in support of that application. That, by itself, is quite unusual. In this case what we are talking about is the two coming together with essentially locked arms, and saying, 'Here we have a proposition that we basically agree with, and support.' "
**Ted Chase, Planning Board Chairman, Lewisboro, NY**

## Step 7: Help gain project approvals

As the project continues through the approvals (permitting) process, the collaborative planning team helps with plan revisions and presentations to the various boards. The project will improve throughout this period as collaboration within the team and between the team and the boards continues to improve. Planning board presentations and meetings are shorter and more pleasant because of the cooperation and teamwork among the parties. Better ideas for selection and placement of community-enhancing features will continue to be identified. Creative solutions for funding the construction and maintenance of communty-enhancing features will also appear.

## Conclusion

Planning board presentations by the collaborative planning team yield extraordinary results! The board is pleased by the participation of all parties. The neighbors get the community-enhancing features they need. The environmentalists get enhancements to the environment because of the project, and the developer gets community support for a profitable project.

> Planning board meetings are shorter and more pleasant because of cooperation between neighbors, developer, and environmentalists.

> "People are willing to talk about their needs and their interests and their ideas, and have respect for the people who own the land, and say, 'Well, it's our community. What if we do it this way?' It gets people involved in the democratic process."
>
> **Audrey O'Connell, Environmental Commission, collaborative planning team, Byram, NJ**

*This guidebook is the coach that helps you succeed!*

The remainder of this guidebook explains how you can succeed with collaborative planning regardless of your project's size, type, or history – even if the participants have been suing each other. The following chapters will help this process work for you.

You probably have some questions now. So, let's move on to Chapter Three: Questions & Answers About Collaborative Planning.

"Having tapped the creativity of the local people, the plans themselves are more responsive to the residents' short and long term needs. The plans are simply more creative in terms of the use of the space and in many cases they're more environmentally sound in taking advantage of existing features."
**Ted Chase, Planning Board Chairman, Select Board, Lewisboro, NY**

# Questions and Answers About Collaborative Planning

## Contents

# Questions and Answers About Collaborative Planning

*"Is it legal for all of us to be enjoying this so much?"*

**1** Is the planning board meeting its state-mandated responsibility by encouraging collaborative planning?

When a collaborative planning team designs a project that integrates well with the surrounding neighborhood and enhances it, the planning board gets a good plan to review. Encouraging and supporting collaborative planning shows that the planning board is meeting state-mandated responsibility to oversee and coordinate good land development planning of the town. The Collaborative Planning guidelines in the Appendix provide town officials with a format for setting up the collaborative planning process. Collaborative planning is a voluntary process that is used to design projects so that they include community-enhancing features.

Collaborative planning gives the planning board a way to coordinate good development of the town.

**2** Could collaborative planning yield "spot zoning?"

The state land use law that authorizes the planning board and gives it the authority to oversee planning in the town and to decide what plans get approved. If the plan does not comply with all the regulations, but the board thinks it is well planned and will blend into and benefit the adjacent neighborhood, they may approve it by variance, waiver, or revising the regulations. When the neighbors support variances for a project because it improves their lives and property values, the project revitalizes the area and the variances do not create "spot zoning" that will get the planning board in trouble.

Plans that integrate with the surrounding neighborhood are not "spot zoning."

**3** How can the planning board find the neighbors of a proposed project at the beginning of the planning process?

Collaborative planning is used in settled areas where the site of the proposed project has people living or working around it. The names and mailing addresses of people living adjacent to a proposed project can be identified from the tax records. The procedure for notifying the neighbors and a sample letter about collaborative planning to be sent to the neighbors are included in the Collaborative Planning guidelines in the Appendix.

Neighbors of proposed projects can be identified and notified from tax records.

**4** Could the planning board lose a lawsuit for not granting a variance for a community-enhancing feature?

A variance requested by a collaborative planning team might include a non-permitted community-enhancing feature. Since each project is a different size, in a different location, involving different community-enhancing features, granting a variance to permit a certain community-enhancing feature in one project is not likely to be seen as justification to grant a variance on another project. The planning board or zoning board or town council has the final say about whether the feature is important enough to community life to grant the variance. If the feature does not clearly enhance community life in the eyes of the planning board when variance is requested, it is unlikely that the collaborative planning team strongly supports that feature and unlikely that a judge would award the variance to the developer in litigation.

Non-permitted community-enhancing features must be clearly justified to receive variances.

"The planning board benefits by having at least a concept to work with that has local community support. In a couple of cases I think it's fairly certain that we've been able to avoid litigation."
*Ted Chase, Planning Board Chairman, Lewisboro, NY*

**Community-enhancing features are sound planning.**

## 5 Could the collaborative planning process result in plans that violate sound planning principles?

There is little risk because the collaborative planning process is used to design projects that (1) include needed community-enhancing features for the settled area and (2) achieve the goals and principles of the master plan and the land development regulations.

**Collaborative planning process is a process for improving relationships. It cannot be used against anybody.**

## 6 Could neighbors use the collaborative planning process against the planning board or developer?

No. The collaborative planning process requires the collaborative participation of the developer. If the developer decides at any time to no longer participate with the neighbors, the collaborative planning process is at an end. Also, the neighbors and developer have no power over the planning board and the existing land development regulations. The planning board approves the project. In fact, it is prudent for the neighbors and developer to keep the planning board well informed as to their progress. See the Appendix for a sample letter that should be sent to the planning board after every collaborative planning session between the developer and neighbors. The collaborative planning process is a way to improve relationships and to gain the benefits from doing so. It cannot be used against anybody.

OH, IT'S ANOTHER UPDATE LETTER FROM OUR COLLABORATIVE PLANNING TEAM.

PLANNING BOARD

**7** With collaborative planning, is there still a public hearing?

Yes. The public hearing process is not changed in any way by using the collaborative planning process.

Yes, with collaborative planning there is still a public hearing.

**8** Is it worthwhile to discuss the collaborative planning process publicly when there is no proposed project?

Yes. When people living in population centers see collaborative planning as a way to design proposed land development projects to solve crime, traffic, and pollution problems and to achieve affordable housing, they gain hope and are not as likely to flee to less developed areas. They also gain confidence in using collaborative planning themselves with the developer of a proposed project. The collaborative planning process is for people in settled areas who are interested in how their community is developing and who might, given the opportunity, participate in an effective process for improving the quality of a proposed land development.

Public discussion about the collaborative planning process gives hope to residents of settled areas.

**9** Wouldn't it be better to keep concerned citizens out of the planning until the public hearing?

No. With collaborative planning, the energy of concerned citizens is redirected to lead the collaboration. As they participate, local citizens realize that, collaboratively, they can efficiently use their energy to improve the proposed project to include community-enhancing features. They find that even on projects that have been confrontational and litigious, they can build an effective, collaborative relationship with town officials and the developer. Research and testimonials show that the sooner the neighbors are involved, the better the collaboration, and the more community-enhancing features are included in the project plan.

"I think this process is perfect for a planning board because the planning board is in the hot seat. I mean the planning board are members of the community and a development comes to a community and sometimes people feel it's being forced down their throat and the planning board is kind of stuck in the middle. This process gives everybody a chance to talk about their own particular needs and work as a team."
*Audrey O'Connell,*
*Environmental Commission,*
*Byram, NJ*

### 10 Are ordinary citizens knowledgeable enough to participate in collaborative planning?

Yes. The collaborative planning process uses a large aerial photo that shows both the project site and its surrounding neighborhood. Ordinary citizens are capable of identifying natural, historic, and cultural places in their neighborhood on the aerial photo. They are also capable of selecting and modeling connecting walkways through the proposed project site, as well as needed recreational facilities, parks,

Neighbors know the community-enhancing features that will help their neighborhood.

and other community-enhancing features that could be included in the project. Ordinary citizens are also good at keeping the focus on building trust among the stakeholders, which is the most important part of designing a community-enhancing project.

**11** **Why not get design ideas from existing projects rather than use collaborative planning?**

There are very few projects that are specifically designed to vitalize their surrounding neighbors. To get those projects we need a process that generates them. The process for creating community-building land development is not simply complying with land use regulations (in the same way the process for creating a good marriage is not simply complying with divorce regulations). To the degree that neighbors, developer, city planners, and environmentalists focus on the process of building one cohesive team, they will design community-enhancing features into their project. We have to rework the project design process to achieve exemplary neighborhood-improving land development.

> Community-building land development needs a community-building design process.

**12** **Why not just educate the public about good design and good questions to ask?**

Those are good ideas, but they have not, generally, been enough to generate neighborhood-enhancing projects. The reasons that proposed projects don't achieve neighborhood-enhancing objectives are (1) the lack of outward focus on including needed community-enhancing features and (2) the lack of teamwork between neighbors, developer, and environmentalists in planning the project. Concerned citizens offer the best energy to achieve these objectives. They need to be supported by the planning board in hosting a collaborative process that improves proposed projects in their neighborhoods.

> When the public leads the collaboration, there is no more confrontation.

> "I think that there are people in every community who will see the need for this process, and I do think this is the only way to do it."
> *Ruth Smith,*
> *collaborative planning team,*
> *Town Council, Planning*
> *Board, Mendham, NJ*

### 13 Is the current public participation process adequate?

The current public participation process is fine, but it is not achieving Smart Growth.

Yes, the current public participation procedure is fine for the land development design and approval system that is in place today. However, projects that solve environmental and societal problems and enhance existing neighborhoods in population centers could be better. Our research shows that collaboration in project design, when combined with a focus on including community-enhancing features in the project, will yield better projects. Collaborative planning is a way to design projects that are appealing to developers and achieve Smart Growth. It does not affect the process for public participation that is used today.

### 14 Don't the zoning regulations dictate land development solutions?

Zoning regulations are still needed with a collaborative project design process.

Simply complying with zoning regulations yields projects that protect the rights of the community, the developer, and the environment. It doesn't seem to be enough to achieve Smart Growth and to stop Sprawl. Good zoning regulations are necessary, just as good divorce regulations are necessary. But, a process that improves the relationships between the stakeholders opens the door to the creativity, flexibility, and teamwork that can solve problems, achieve Smart Growth, and end Sprawl. Collaborative planning is a voluntary process, like a marriage, that needs to be backed up by good regulations in the event that the parties cannot work together.

**15** Since the public usually doesn't want development, won't their involvement just aggravate things?

In collaborative planning the concerned citizens use their energy to host collaborative meetings with the developer, city planner, and environmentalists. Together, they select the appropriate community-enhancing features and obtain community support and resources for including these features in the project. The concerned citizens and developer together present their community-enhancing project to the planning board for approvals. The public's new focus on leading the collaborative effort changes aggravation into community building.

Neighbors leading collaboration ends confrontation.

"Every planning board should consider this process from this standpoint: They need all the help they can get!"
*William M. Cox, Attorney, Author of New Jersey Zoning and Land Use Administration*

**16** Shouldn't the neighbors' views be subordinate to the law?

Stakeholders' views about density and land use are subordinate to the law.

Yes, the neighbors' views, as well as the developer's and everyone else's views, are subordinate to the law. The neighbors' views about density and land use are not their primary focus in collaborative planning. The neighbors' job is to set up and maintain a collaborative process with the developer and, as a team, to determine the best community-enhancing features to include in the project, find the necessary resources, and present the community-enhancing project to the planning board.

**17** How will people ever agree on a plan that is good for the neighborhood?

Stakeholder differences yield creative problem-solving and community-enhancing features.

Those very differences, plus the collaborative forum, are what generate the creativity to solve previously unsolvable environmental and societal problems. Most people seem to agree on community-enhancing features. The most important work in collaborative planning is teambuilding. People with different and divergent views who live in the same area find they still have much in common and can become friends. Energized by their team spirit, neighbors and developer configure the plan to include the appropriate community-enhancing features and find the resources to build it.

**18** Does the collaborative planning process represent the wishes of non-participating residents?

The community-enhancing features that the participants select may not represent the wishes of the non-participating residents. However, the collaborative team effort seems to generate solutions that are widely appealing. In addition, neighborhood residents know that anyone is always welcome to join in the planning at any time. Some area residents attend a few meetings until they are comfortable that the process being followed will lead to sensible decisions.

> The collaboration yields community-enhancing features that appeal to most people.

**19** Can the collaborative planning process make it easier for officials to encourage increased density in population centers?

IT WILL STOP SPRAWL!
IT WILL SOLVE PROBLEMS!
IT WILL INCREASE YOUR PROPERTY VALUE!
THE DEVELOPERS WILL LOVE IT AND SO WILL YOU!

> Denser development in population centers can be a community-enhancing feature.

Town officials can encourage collaborative planning because development projects that are designed with it will appeal to residents, solve problems, increase property values, and work for the developer. The collaborative planning process is something new that works politically – all stakeholders like it – and it just happens to generate projects that revitalize population centers so residents don't want to flee to Sprawl projects.

> "From my experience on the planning board and town council, I think that it's not possible to legislate the diversity that is needed in our community. The planning board will ultimately have total control over this process, but it will still allow for a real mix of units where the planning board thinks that's desirable."
>
> **Ruth Smith,**
> **Planning Board,**
> **Town Council,**
> **Mendham, NJ**

## GLOSSARY OF IMPORTANT WORDS

Those are some questions that arise when people are first introduced to collaborative planning. In addition, this is a good place to review some words that are part of the changing paradigm regarding land development. As we expand our thinking, familiar terms take on new shades of meaning, and new words are needed to communicate new ideas. Here is an alphabetical listing of the more important words and their meanings as used in this book.

### Agenda

Two meanings are used in this book: (1) a list of items to cover in a meeting and (2) a mind-set that is focused on achieving a special-interest goal. In meaning number 2, people in the roles of developer, neighbor, environmentalist, and municipal official each have their own mind-set agendas. Their mind-set agenda is the result of their land development experience. The Smarter Land Use project has discovered that an overall community-building agenda exists that includes within it the special-interest agendas of the neighbors, developers, environmentalists, and officials. It turns out that by designing the project together to achieve the community-building agenda, neighbors, developer, environmentalists, and officials have the best opportunity to achieve their special-interest agendas. And it is a lot more enjoyable!

### Collaboration

The working relationship when people with different areas of expertise design a project together as one cohesive team. Rather than promoting their individual agendas in stereotypical ways, team members share their expertise. The greater the friendship and trust among the participants, the more effective the collaboration. The more effective the collaboration, the more wholesome and unifying is the project that they design.

### Collaborative Planning Process

A step-by-step process for (1) building a unified team with the neighbors, developer, city planner, and environmentalists involved in a particular proposed project, and then (2) designing a financially feasible land development project expressly to enhance the surrounding neighborhood by including community-enhancing features and solving environmental and societal problems. This process has been detailed by the Smarter Land Use Project.

## Collaborative planning team

An open, inclusive, voluntary group of several interested citizens predominantly residing in proximity to the proposed project, and including the developer, other interested citizens, and local planning staff where feasible. The objective of the collaborative planning team is to design the land development concept plan that is most beneficial to the surrounding community and economically satisfactory to the landowner/developer.

## Consensus

A collective opinion or general agreement. True consensus of a group is developed through complete participation and creative involvement from every member of the group. See the Consensus Checklist in the Appendix.

## Expertise

Knowledge and understanding of a specific subject usually accompanied by experience. As in "Expertise in land development, environmental factors, and neighborhood conditions is essential in designing the best land development in a particular neighborhood."

## Land Development

Improving the function of a particular parcel of land so that it has greater value to life in its sphere of influence. This almost always involves a new use with a greater human presence and additional construction by humans on the parcel.

## Land Use

The function served by a particular parcel of land. The functions served by a piece of property may involve humans changing the natural environment, or they may prohibit such human intervention. A wide range of human interventions with the natural environment may achieve the chosen land use. The process for making land use decisions is an important factor in the health of our environment, our economy, and our society.

### Master Plan (also known as a Comprehensive Plan)

A vision of the best long term use for all the land in a particular political jurisdiction. Determining the best long term land use is difficult and involves an ongoing dynamic process requiring meaningful broad-based citizen participation. One element of the master plan is to specify a process for updating it that includes citizen involvement and support.

### Master Plan Update Procedure (MPUP)

Every town periodically updates its master plan. It is helpful to use an update procedure based on collaborative planning that has broad-based citizen ownership and support of the master plan vision while complying with current legal requirements. The collaborative planning process recommended by the Smarter Land Use Project has the Master Plan Committee participate with members of the public to update the master plan so that it best solves existing social and environmental problems and enhances community life. Collaborative master planning builds community spirit and thereby allows for inclusion of major community-enhancing features because controversy is reduced (see Chapter Seven).

### Mediation

When people with conflicting agendas focus on finding a compromise solution with which they can live. Mediation in land development generally does not focus on achieving the overall community-building agenda. The larger focus allows the stakeholders to achieve their special-interest agendas. Collaborative planning is not mediation. Rather, it helps communities reach a higher level of cooperation where mediation is not required.

## Paradigm for land development

The set of assumptions or beliefs that governs the thinking and mentality of people who are actively involved in making land development decisions.

## Paradigm shift in land development

When some of the assumptions that have been guiding land development are replaced with new assumptions that result in better land development and healthier communities.

## Permitting Process

The process for gaining local, county, and state approvals of the detailed project design plans. After the plans have been approved by all relevant agencies, a building permit is granted by the municipality. Cooperation between neighbors, planning board, developer, and environmentalists makes this process faster, easier, and more pleasant.

## Planning Board (also called a Planning Commission)

A group of dedicated citizens, usually serving without pay, who serve their community by overseeing and coordinating the development of its land. Their time is usually spent reviewing developers' plans and recommending improvements in the land use regulations. They sometimes find themselves caught in the middle between neighbors of a proposed project who don't like the project, the developer who is complying with the regulations, and environmental advocates.

## Proposed Project

When a real estate property in a settled area is for sale and a developer is interested in improving it for commercial, residential, or recreational use. A proposed project may be in the form of a development concept, a preliminary plan, or a detailed plan approved for construction. The design of proposed projects in settled areas will generally benefit from collaborative planning.

**Radburn**

An ungated, residential land development in Fairlawn, New Jersey, which demonstrates an extraordinary sense of safety and community, as well as complete socio-economic diversity. Each home is connected to the central park and the surrounding community via public, paved walkways. (See Chapter Six for aerial photos and a complete description of Radburn.)

**Reconciliation**

The realization or restoration of trust, harmony and friendship between people with different areas of expertise. Reconciliation precedes collaboration (after people make friends, they can collaborate). Reconciliation in land development may be needed among neighbors, developer, environmentalists, and city officials. Each player has different expertise that is essential in achieving good land development. As they reconcile and become friends, they can collaborate to design projects that also build community spirit.

**Settled Area**

A place of concentrated human activity where a proposed land development or redevelopment project usually has at least a dozen neighbors living or working in close proximity. In settled areas, proposed land development is characterized as infill, redevelopment, or fringe development. Existing land development in settled areas may be characterized as urban, suburban, rural village, or sprawl.

**Smarter Land Use**

Individual projects in settled areas that have been designed expressly to solve existing environmental and societal problems and enhance life in the surrounding neighborhood. Smarter land use generally results from a collaborative planning process.

## Smart Growth

An expansion of human activity that solves existing societal and environmental problems and enhances community life. Smart Growth projects build community spirit, solve existing problems, and further develop the best character and identity of the area. They increase property values and reduce the expense of community services. They are generally supported by both residents and developers and may be more easily approved. The collaborative planning process described herein is one way to achieve Smart Growth.

## Sprawl

The expansion of settled areas in ways that aggravate existing societal and environmental problems. Sprawl evolves when land development projects are not expressly designed to enhance their adjacent neighborhoods. Sprawl is aggravated by inward focus on the project itself and by distrust and confrontation between the developer, the public, and city planners. Since it is unlikely that development will enhance an undeveloped area, projects built in unsettled areas, where they do not have at least a dozen immediately adjacent neighbors, generally contribute to Sprawl.

## CHAPTER FOUR

# How to Work with the Developer

## Contents

# How to Work with the Developer

*So... how **do** we make friends and find community-enhancing solutions?*

### Success — Franklin, New Jersey
### Conflict: Commercial use adjacent to residential area.
### Solution: Relationships improved. Walkways and park added.

*In Franklin, a lawsuit was threatened because a home for the aged planned to expand into a residential neighborhood. The collaborative planning team broke through an impenetrable wall of past hostility and undergrowth between the residential neighborhood and the home for the aged to create a park where the older people and the neighbors could meet, sit, and enjoy each other.*

"When I got the letter, I was horrified. As a neighbor, I enjoyed this piece of property so much. We had lost in court the last time with this developer, and felt a sense of frustration. Because of the history there was a lot of suspicion and the idea that we could cooperate together was not taken seriously by anybody. Somebody had heard of this collaborative process so, since nothing else was working, we called.

Everyone was very skeptical and guarded when we started. The collaborative planning process was completely different from the past because it looked to our common interests. Without ever really talking to the developer, you picture him as some kind of a big, bad monster that's out to ruin you and they don't care about you. So to actually get to know them, you realize, wow, that this is a great thing, that they are not something you imagined that's really terrible, but these are people that really have a need to do the project.

As soon as we got to know them better, I realized that they did not want to have another big legal battle any more than we did, even though they had more bucks than us. That meant that there was more good faith that we could expect on their part. We spent time getting comfortable with one another and building a relationship where we could move forward together. It was amazing to see us actually working together. I thought, 'This is more than I prayed for!' That's how impressed I was. I just thought, 'Wow, this is really, really great to see people coming together.' It was just a wonderful experience. After the past, I really couldn't even believe it.

The feeling at the board meeting was extremely positive. In addition to agreeing on the plan, we had added connecting sidewalks, a park, and a trail. The board was very impressed.

The most important thing was the time spent initially thinking about possibilities for improving the area. We didn't get into it as much as we could have. We couldn't believe it could happen here. We just were thinking too small. There is a lot more room for cooperation than you ever dream. We get so fixated on our own interests and the potential for conflict that it becomes a recipe for head-butting and we miss the fact that there is a huge common ground."

**Pat and Dana Cochran,
collaborative planning participants**

"This process brought the people together. Meeting in different homes, touring the site together, and getting to know each other was very helpful. We were very pleased with the results and we hope that the relationships that were established continue into the future."

**Jim Stahl, Developer and Attorney**

*The collaborative planning team scratching and looking for ticks after breaking through the wall.*

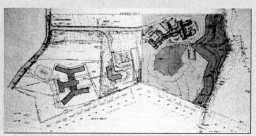

*Proposed addition is in the upper right.*

# How to Work with the Developer

## Introduction

Regardless of past experience, neighbors, developers, planners, and environmentalists usually want to work together.

After participating in hundreds of meetings with neighbors, developers, planners, and environmentalists, I have learned that they all want very much to cooperate. Even when their recent experiences with each other have been hostile, they will usually collaborate enthusiastically if they have a comfortable setting, a potentially productive meeting agenda, and the instructions and tools presented in this book. Working together toward a common goal then brings out the best in everyone.

## Hints for Creating a Cohesive Team

Here are the hints we have found most helpful in creating a cohesive team.

Begin the collaborative planning process with a few meetings that include just the neighbors.

1. Begin the collaborative planning process with a few meetings that include just the neighbors. Gather materials, learn about collaborative planning, recruit additional participants, and make the decision to start. Then invite the city planners, environmentalists and other interested citizens, followed by the developer. Starting the process this way welcomes the developer in as an invited, key member of a functioning, collaborative planning team whose meetings are hosted by the neighbors.

2. Sunday afternoon is a good time for the first meeting that includes neighbors, developer, city planner and environmentalists and any other people who might want to participate. People tend to be relaxed, sociable, and attentive.

3. Make the decision to collaborate with a show of hands so that each person can see that the others have also decided to cooperate and work as a team. Make the collaboration decision an agenda item.

4. Sit around a comfortable, well-lit dining room table in a neighbor's home, on which is placed the map or aerial photo that shows the site and its surrounding neighborhood. It works well when meetings are held in the neighborhood adjacent to the project site. However, collaboration can certainly also succeed if meetings are held in other locations.

*Neighbors host meetings to design a project that enhances their neighborhood.*

5.  In situations where people seem wedded to confrontational agendas or certain roles or "hats," give two stick-on name tags to each participant: A name label on which they print their first name large and a "hat label" on which they print whether they are a developer, neighbor, city planner, environmentalist, etc. After introductions and an explanation, each participant ceremoniously strips off their "hat label" and deposits it in a wastepaper basket.

*To help participants realize their underlying common goal, they ceremoniously strip off their "hat" labels.*

"The big issue was that no one was talking to anybody. I mean feelings were that hurt! And, you can't really go forward and build a community if you have no community that's willing to talk. So getting people just talking together about their needs and different ways of solving their needs was obviously the first step."
**Audrey O'Connell, collaborative planning team, Environmental Commission, Byram, New Jersey**

6.	Serve light refreshments or maybe even offer a potluck meal before you begin meetings. Allow time at the beginning and the end of each meeting to gather around the refreshments and get to know each other better.

7.	Adopt a written agenda when you start each meeting. See the Appendix for samples. People relax when they know what is coming, that they are on schedule, and when the meeting will end.

8	Copy the Consensus Checklist as presented in the Appendix onto the reverse side of every meeting agenda. It contains the most important rules to keep in mind during meetings to allow creative collaboration to happen. After introductions, ask each participant to read out loud one item from the Consensus Checklist. Invite anyone to reference it at any time during the meeting to help encourage collaborative, productive discussion.

The Consensus Checklist in the Appendix contains the most important guidelines to effective collaboration. Copy it on the back of every meeting agenda.

*Copy the Consensus Checklist in the Appendix onto the back of every meeting agenda.*

9. Try for equal numbers of men and women and a variety of ages participating. People gain confidence to speak up when they are in the presence of their peers.

10. Invite young people, age 12 and older, to be on the team. They tend to encourage team cooperation. They also are alert to what the neighborhood needs. They round out the team and can add a wholesome quality to the discussion. Remember, the project being planned will ultimately be used by our children and their children.

11. Set up a meeting or meetings for all participants to tour the development site and the surrounding neighborhood. Walking tours are great opportunities to get to know each other and share ideas. Along the way be sure to take time to walk and talk with every person you don't know very well.

12. At every meeting when the participants introduce themselves, have them share something new and good in their personal lives. This lifts each person's and the group's consciousness from possible anxiety about the meeting to good news. It also gives people something good to discuss when they get time to make friends. It is a helpful exercise to get each meeting off to a positive start.

> Walking tours of the site and neighborhood are great opportunities to get to know each other and to share ideas.

At each meeting give every person time to share something new and good in their personal life.

> "We have all these interests. Let's talk about them. Let's make it all work because we believe in the end we can make it work, and we believe we can build a better community."
> **Audrey O'Connell, collaborative planning team, Environmental Commission, Byram, New Jersey**

13. During modeling the participants each share about a time and place where they experienced a strong feeling of community or belonging, for example a certain neighborhood party, vacation place, or reunion. Ask them to be specific and describe the situation.

Sharing community experiences is fun and sets the stage for including community-enhancing features.

14. Before closing every meeting, ask each person to mention something they appreciate about the person on their right, and about the meeting in general. This gives everyone good, shared memories of the meeting and of their own personal contribution to it. It encourages people to come back for another enjoyable, productive experience.

15. Always sit in a circle. Try to keep the circle just one row deep. As more representatives of the developer, environmentalists, neighbors, and the community begin to participate, simply widen the circle and keep it one row deep if possible.

16. Encourage people to warmly welcome newcomers at all times and always sit next to and try to make friends with a person they don't know well, or even one they currently dislike!

SIT NEXT TO SOMEONE YOU DON'T CURRENTLY LIKE.

17. Consider adopting a policy where everyone speaks once before anyone speaks twice. In community building, an idea that at first seems very insignificant and out of place can result in a permanent, valuable contribution to the project and the community. For the best community-enhancing plans to emerge, thoughts from everyone need to be encouraged, heard, appreciated, and recorded.

"There's nothing wrong with having needs and being willing to speak about our needs and someone else's needs and saying, 'Okay, yeah, I have to recognize your rights too.' and 'Hey, this is a team.' I mean, you know, life is teamwork. So, in that sense it helps anybody."

*Audrey O'Connell, collaborative planning team, Environmental Commission, Byram, New Jersey*

Don't focus
discussion on
existing ordinances.

18. Don't focus discussion on existing ordinances or regulations. Collaboration is about shared creativity to achieve the best community-enhancing project. Ultimately, the regulations will have to be met. However, discussion about regulatory requirements should be minimized because it stifles the creativity and collaboration needed to optimize community-enhancing land development. It is best to postpone discussion about regulations until the planning board meetings.

19. Meetings cannot have too many or too few participants to be productive as a team. To make it possible for everyone to contribute ideas, when there are twelve or more participants, create sub-groups of five to seven participants to work on the same or different tasks on the agenda.

*Meetings cannot have too many or too few participants.*

20. Allow participants to express their feelings and concerns, sometimes known as "venting." It is important to focus on the goodness of the person who is expressing their feelings rather than what they are saying, and to listen with patience and compassion. Avoid telling the person that they need not or should not feel that way.

*Listen with patience and compassion.*

## Keep the Focus on Team-Building

Each concept that causes confrontation can also become a catalyst for community building. Discussion of sizable features can cause sizable conflict. The energy invested in conflict can always be switched to community building. It takes courage for the proponents of a particular feature to decide to concentrate their energy on building trust and cooperation and team spirit with their perceived opponents – rather than pushing for or defending against a pre-conceived notion.

Community building is not achieved by selling your idea to the group, by effectively defending yourself against someone else's idea, nor by compromise or fault finding. Rather, it is achieved by using all your energy to help create one cohesive and spirited team and then sharing ideas and helping to implement the best ideas as a member of that team. Team spirit works like magic to solve previously

> Community building is not achieved by selling your idea to the group.

"No one's needs are more important than anybody else's needs. We put that out there, and got people working toward feeling comfortable with that statement. This process brings up those fuzzy issues of ownership, and stewardship, and inter-dependence, and team-work."

*Audrey O'Connell,*
*collaborative planning team,*
*Environmental Commission,*
*Byram, New Jersey*

unsolvable problems and build a better community. You cannot overdose on team spirit. The more the better. Important ideas that would have been withheld due to fear of confrontation are shared when there is team spirit. The better a team is working together, the better the community-enhancing features they find a way to include. The idea you anxiously want to defend may ultimately be selected, or something better may emerge and even you will abandon the feature you were originally advocating.

> The better the team is working together, the better the community-enhancing features they find a way to include.

*You cannot overdose on team spirit. The more the better.*

## Succeed by Seeing the Good

To be an effective participant in collaborative planning requires nothing more than appreciating and acknowledging something good in what other people are saying or doing. That is all that needs to be done. By appreciating and acknowledging something good in every idea that is presented, the participant encourages more good ideas to be presented.

Focusing on what is good is also very relaxing, freeing, and creative for both the presenter and the listener. It is helpful to allow people to express negative feelings. Still, the listener tries to see the good in the person as they are expressing the negative feelings. Don't focus on the negative feelings; just listen respectfully. Simply expressing their feelings will help the speaker feel better. Don't agree with or disagree with or discount the negative feelings. Just listen to the speaker with compassion and understanding, while you are thinking good thoughts about them. Be appreciative, see the good in them, thank them, and move on.

Seeing the good in each other will encourage good ideas. This process will resolve conflicts and insure that the best community-enhancing features are included in the plan. If the team is having problems getting the best community-enhancing features included in the plan, check to see if each member is focused on seeing the good in every idea and in every person participating.

> Just appreciating something good in each comment made by the other participants will yield a community-enhancing project.

> If the team is having problems, focus on what is good.

> "It got people involved. It got them to delineate their interests or talk about their interests and it got them to come to solutions about what would help them. When we put it together as a whole unit – and now we work as that whole unit – we're helping everybody else."
>
> *Audrey O'Connell, collaborative planning team, Environmental Commission, Byram, New Jersey*

### Take Off the Masks

*An important team activity is to help participants come out from behind their masks.*

One idea that helps people achieve collaboration is for them to realize that when they look at another person they are seeing a mask that has to do with that person's life experiences and the roles they play. Our research shows that under every mask is a cooperative person who wants to come out. A major activity of the collaborative planning team is to help each member out from under their mask. Sometimes it helps to imagine the person under the mask playing with their children. To build team spirit, solve problems, build community, and design great projects, keep all discussion and activities at the meetings between the people under the masks, not just between masks. Take off the masks and enjoy the magic that results.

*Behind every mask is a cooperative person who wants to come out. Take off the masks and enjoy the magic!*

## Difficult Situations

In spite of all the hints and ideas presented above, unforeseen and difficult situations do arise. When that happens my suggestion is to sit back, breathe deeply, and wait. Someone usually comes up with a good idea and the team continues to move forward. Below you will find two examples.

### Dealing with a Problem Participant

Occasionally, a person who does not like collaboration comes to a meeting defending a personal agenda. If that person has outstanding timing, he or she can create havoc and destroy team spirit just as it begins to gain a foothold. I had this experience with a person in one group. It was very exasperating and discouraging. Meeting after meeting this person would arrive, sit relatively quietly until the perfect moment, then with well-timed words he would destroy the teamwork and spirit achieved by the participants. This problem was solved when we met in a small room where this person had to be physically close to other people. Somehow this ruined his sense of timing. As a result his comments no longer made any sense, and the solidarity of the group could not be broken by his words. He left the meeting and never returned.

> Meet in the smallest room that will accommodate the team with the map or aerial photo on a table in the center, with chairs for the participants, and have refreshments available.

> "There were difficult times in the early stages as trust was gradually established between the developer, the town administrative representatives, and the local residents. That kind of trust takes a while to develop and there were times when people said, 'Oh shucks, it's not going to work.' But there was always the promise of something very, very worthwhile coming out of it, that they could feel they were a part of."
> **Ted Chase,**
> **collaborative planning team,**
> **Planning Board Chairman,**
> **Lewisboro, NY**

Visiting Radburn
helped the parties
settle a lawsuit with
an *improved* project
rather than a
compromise.

### Lawsuit in Progress

A developer had filed suit against a town for changing the zoning in the middle of his application. It was a bitter lawsuit. The mayor took the collaborative planning process to the judge as a possible solution. The developer was present at the discussion and agreed to participate in a few meetings at the judge's suggestion. The developer, neighbors, and town officials separately visited Radburn, a model development described in Chapter Five. They were each impressed with that model for the project. They started collaborative planning with the support of the town council, and once they had begun the process, both parties stayed with it and relations improved until the suit settled about six months later. The settlement included a park, recreation facilities, connecting walkways, and affordable housing. In addition there was a compromise in density that favored the town. The developer became quite excited about the community-enhancing project that evolved.

## Collaboration Is Essential in Land Development – and It Works

The better people get
along and work
together, the better
the project they plan.

The better people get along and work together, the better the project they plan. It works! Why? Through the years I have thought about that question a lot. I have concluded that collaboration is the inherent nature of human beings. It is our natural way of being. When we are not collaborating, we are coping with some fear. By taking the step to start collaborating, we face the fear, deal with it, and no longer need to cope by not collaborating. That's why collaboration is so fulfilling.

Ironically, we find support to start collaborating in our perceived adversaries. I have found in the last twelve years researching this project that almost everyone – developers, planners, environmentalists, neighbors – is interested in working together if the other one will. In most cases I was introduced to situations when there was already substantial confrontation and distrust. It was a matter of setting up a situation where the perceived adversaries could meet informally and take the necessary steps to start collaborating. I tried a number of different steps, forums, and tools. They all worked to some degree. What you are seeing here is the best so far. There are certainly better ideas out there. If you know of one that has worked for you, please let me know and I will share it on the website or in the next edition of this book. We are all in this together, and I think we all have the urge to cooperate. You don't need to believe me, just try it. Think about your biggest adversary in land use. Would you try collaboration if they would?

## A Hands-On Project Helps Collaboration

Collaboration is much easier to achieve when the perceived opponents are focused on doing a hands-on project together. A joint hands-on project helps because they are looking at something else besides each other, and because it gives them a common goal. I found that an aerial photo of the project site that also includes the surrounding neighborhood is a great aid in collaborating. When the parties work together to build a scale model of the project right on the aerial photo, it is like hitting a home run with collaboration. The next chapter shows you how to get the aerial photo and the modeling materials, and how to use them effectively.

Almost everyone – developers, planners, environmentalists, neighbors – is interested in working together if the other one will.

Collaboration is easier to achieve when the perceived opponents are focused on doing a project together.

"People's feelings were hurt in the two years before and so we had to mend some fences and push on. We had to work through some hostility and some bad feelings and get people to really talk and kind of forget about that and say, 'Well, where do we go from here?' If we sit and say, 'I'm hurt, I'm cranky – and I don't want to play,' well, that's fine, but there's not going to be a gain then. In the end there is going to be a development. So, let's try to make it the best development for all of us."

*Audrey O'Connell, collaborative planning team, Environmental Commission, Byram, New Jersey*

# Aerial Photos and Project Modeling Materials

## Contents

# Aerial Photos and Project Modeling Materials

*"With these models on the aerial photo, it is easier to understand what you mean and for us to try new ideas and improve the plan."*
**—Developer**

## Success — Bloomfield, New Jersey
### Conflict: Between residents and officials over brownfields site.
### Solution: Relations improved.

In Bloomfield, residents who lived in the neighborhood surrounding a brownfields (contaminated) site were very upset with town officials. The collaborative planning team used the aerial photo, modeling materials, and collaboration techniques in more than twenty meetings to improve relations with town officials and set a positive direction.

"When we began this process the neighborhood was focused on crime problems and the contamination of a major local property. Dialogue with officials was non-existent or strained at best.

Now, after many meetings, citizens of the immediate area have achieved credibility and respect with town officials and also with other town residents. We did this in group meetings by encouraging people to participate. The visioning process with the aerial photo allowed us to see that we could make the neighborhood better. The process expanded from very local to town-wide to officials. We met regularly to discuss land use and the focus evolved into relationship building. Now I can disagree with people and have them disagree with me and still maintain a level of comradeship and respect instead of annihilation and non-communication. We have established a collaborative process where the politicians have been drawn to participate. That is a very big deal here. There is an energy that is happening now that people are paying attention to improving their areas. This process has helped seed that pride, and that we are all in it together. It's gotten people talking again who verbally hated each other, and it's still happening."
**Carolyn Vadala, collaborative planning team**

"Through this process we have improved relationships between residents and public officials and taken hostility out of the moves that are being made in regard to the contaminated property."
**Vincent Esposito,**
**Councilman at Large**

"The best part of this process for Bloomfield is that it allowed us to really learn from each other. We shared information about how we achieved our goals and overcame obstacles. We now have a successful Executive Committee of Neighborhood Associations that has forged a working relationship with the mayor."
**Susana Sotillo, collaborative planning team**

"This process is empowering everyone involved! All interested and talented parties are now at the table. People with dissimilar frames of reference have been brought together with a common goal: to build a better Bloomfield. Lack of communication and stereotypical views are being overcome. This team effort is beneficial because the end goal is a better place to live now and in the future, for everyone!"

**Nabeelah Abdul-Ghafur,**
**collaborative planning team**

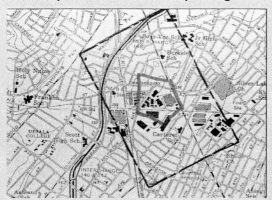
The brownfield site in an urban area

The Bloomfield collaborative planning team.

## Introduction

The first thing you need is a map or an aerial photo that shows both the project site and the surrounding neighborhood. The map or aerial photo must show enough of the surrounding neighborhood that it looks approximately like a donut, with the hole being the project site and the surrounding neighborhood being the donut. This can be done with maps. However, maps don't usually show the locations of buildings or ball fields or walkways. Those features have to be added by hand as part of the modeling process. The deluxe way to model a community-enhancing project is to use an aerial photo. Often you can obtain a large aerial photo of your site and neighborhood at the correct scale at a surprisingly low cost.

> **Get a three foot by five foot map or aerial photo that shows the project site and the neighborhood donut.**

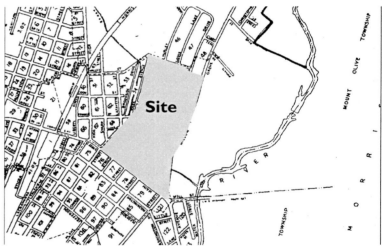

*Make a map of the site and the donut.*

## The Aerial Photo

An aerial photo showing the project site and its surrounding neighborhood helps everyone understand how the site fits into and connects with the neighborhood. An aerial photo also makes it easy to locate and identify important natural, historic, and cultural features. It is easy to work together productively around a large aerial photo. Everyone can find and mark specific homes, recreational facilities, streams, schools, workplaces, and walkways, and see their relative sizes and distances from each other. Because it is a photo, people also have confidence in its accuracy.

> **Because it is a photo people have confidence in its accuracy.**

*It is easy to work together productively around a large aerial photo.*

**The best scale shows the site and the donut on a 40 x 60 inch photo.**

Forty by sixty inch aerial photos showing the site and neighborhood at the most useful scale are readily obtainable from existing negatives in most developing areas. These large aerial photos allow the neighbors, developer, city planner, and environmentalists to model different development configurations directly on the aerial photo with the surrounding neighborhood in full view. This size photo fits nicely on a dining room table.

**State and county agencies may provide large aerial photos at the correct scale at minimal cost.**

Recent aerial photos already exist for most developing areas and are generally available in a forty by sixty inch size with one to two week delivery. Sometimes a branch of the state government has the negatives and will print the photo you want at the size and scale you want at no charge or a minimal charge. Sometimes a private aerial survey company has negatives and will print one for you for a few hundred dollars. Check in the yellow pages, or with your city, county, or state planning department, a local civil engineer, or on the internet to find existing aerial photography of your neighborhood and the site.

"So we all sat around the map and got creative on how we could minimize the effect of traffic to the two areas of the neighborhood and at the same time allow the developer to build houses."

**Audrey O'Connell,
collaborative planning team,
Byram, New Jersey**

# How to Obtain the Aerial Photo and Outline the Site on the Aerial Photo

## Step 1: Get a Map of the Development Site

From the town hall, planning commission office, or landowner, get a map that shows the development site boundaries. It can be a "tax" map or a property survey map from the landowner or from the developer's proposed plan. It is best if it includes dimensions, but not necessary. It can be of any size.

**Tip**

Find out what other adjacent parcels are owned by the same landowner, or under contract by the same developer. You may want to include them in your planning.

From the planning department, get the zoning map for the entire town or section of town. You will be able to see the development site in its larger context.

*The map should show site boundaries and nearby roads.*

## Step 2: Outline the Site on a Street Map

Get a local street map and mark the site boundaries on it. It could be the town zoning map. Make sure the map shows the major streets, railroads, ponds, and streams in the area. They will help you identify the location of your site on the USGS Quad Sheet.

Locate and mark the development site as precisely as you can and notice the relationship of the site to neighboring major roadways, neighborhoods, ponds, and streams.

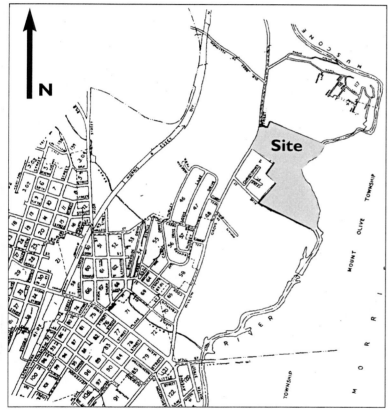

*Outline your site accurately on the street map.*

### Tip
Notice which direction on the map is north, and make a north arrow on the map near the site.

## Step 3: Get the Correct USGS Quad Sheet for Preliminary Topographic and Wetlands Information

From the city planner or other government agency, get a USGS Quadrangle Sheet that includes the development site. You can also buy these at a local map store which you can find in the Yellow Pages, or from the internet. To get the correct Quad Sheet, you or the map store will use the index for your state. They cost about $20.

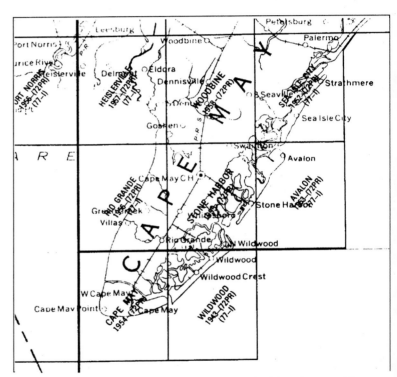

*This is a portion of the Quad Sheet index for New Jersey. Map stores that sell Quad Sheets have the index. Buy the Quad Sheet that includes your site and its surrounding neighborhood. If your site is on the edge, you may have to buy two Quad Sheets.*

## Step 4: Find the Site on the USGS Quad Sheet

Find your development site on the USGS Quad Sheet. The site outlined on the street map below is somewhere on the Quad Sheet on the following page. See if you can find it.

**Tip**
USGS Quad Sheets always have North at the top of the map. Place your map next to the Quad Sheet and find the location of your site.

When you outline your site on a copy of the Quad Sheet, be as accurate as possible.

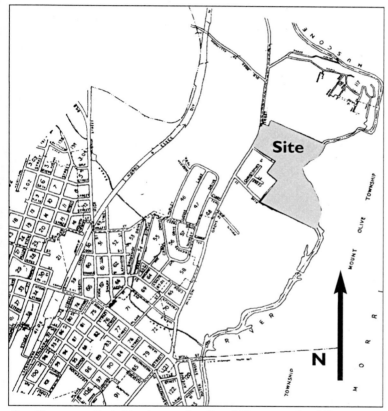

*See if you can find this site on the Quad Sheet on the following page.*

USGS Quad Sheets are 20" by 28" and cover about 60 square miles. They are readily available and are the best way to describe the boundaries of a requested aerial photo to the aerial photography company.

**Tip**
Planners, engineers and realtors usually have a full set of USGS maps for their area. Also, check with your town planning department.

You will send a copy of the portion of the Quad Sheet with your requested photo outlined to the aerial photography company.

Don't forget to tell the photo company the name of the Quad Sheet and the state.

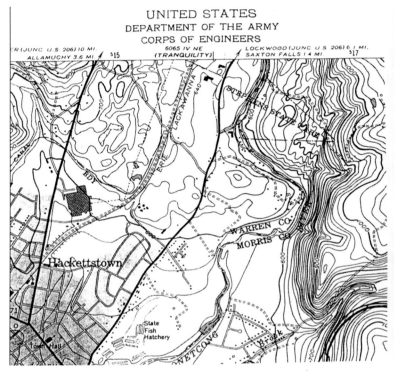

*Can you find the site outlined on the preceding page?*

This is a small portion of Quad Sheet called Hackettstown, NJ. It is shown here full size. The curving lines are contour lines. When they are close together, the slopes are steep. The USGS maps you buy are in color, which helps in recognizing water and woodlands.

Look at the street map on the preceding page and find the lines that represent the roads, river, and railroad. Now find the same roads, river, and railroad on the Quad Sheet. Can you now see where the site is located? It is outlined on the next page.

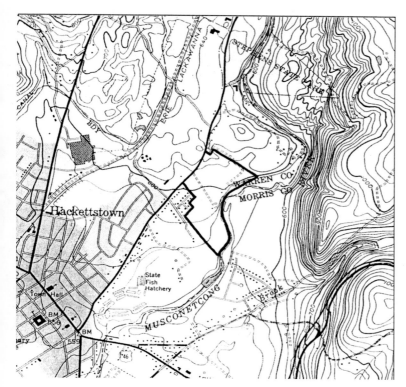

*Here is the site from page 89 outlined on the Quad Sheet.*

**Tip**
Notice the significant development and natural features adjacent to your site. Make sure they are included within your aerial photo borders.

## Step 5: Outline Your Aerial Photo on the Quad Sheet

Select the scale of your 40 x 60 inch aerial photo. The Appendix and the Collaborative Planning Kit have model buildings and recreation facility templates at three scales: 1" =30', 1" = 50', and 1" = 100'. Overlay the three photo scales over your site on the Quad Sheet and see which one shows the surrounding neighborhood best. If you copy this page onto a transparency it is easy to overlay the rectangles onto the Quad Sheet to get the boundaries of your aerial photo.

### Tip

You can make your 40 x 60 inch aerial photo at other scales depending on the size of your site (making sure you include the surrounding neighborhoods). However, the building sizes in the Collaborative Planning Kit may not match the buildings on the aerial photo quite as well for modeling the project.

Keep the photo size at 40 x 60 inches so you can work on it together.

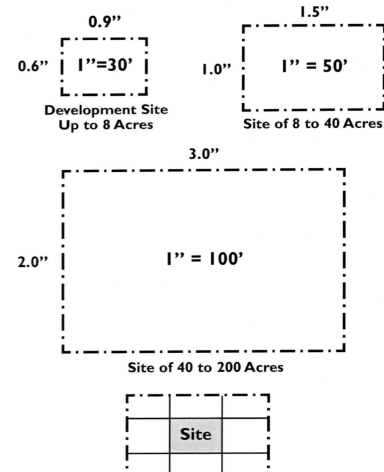

**Size of 40 x 60 inch Aerial Photo When Drawn on Quad Sheet**

0.9"
0.6"  1"=30'
**Development Site Up to 8 Acres**

1.5"
1.0"  1" = 50'
**Site of 8 to 40 Acres**

3.0"
2.0"  1" = 100'
**Site of 40 to 200 Acres**

Site

*Keep plenty of surrounding neighborhood "donut" in your aerial photo. The objective of the collaborative planning process is to develop the site to most enhance the surrounding neighborhood.*

## Step 6: If You Order Your Aerial Photo

This is what you will include with your order to the aerial photo company. They need the boundaries of your requested photo outlined; they don't need the outline of the site. They do need the aerial photo size you want (40" x 60") and the scale (1" = 100') which is confirmed by the boundaries of the photo that you have outlined on the Quad Sheet.

**Tip**
Make your photo outline on an 8.5" x 11" copy of the appropriate portion of the Quad Sheet. You can easily FAX it to the aerial photo company for a price quote and include it with your order.

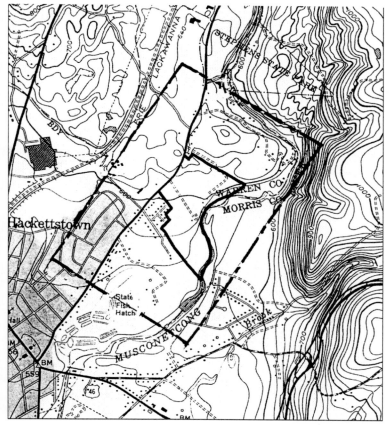

*Include a map like this with your order letter and check.*

**Tip**
Make your Quad Sheet photo outline before you contact an aerial photo company. When you give them the Quad Sheet description of the area you want, they will know immediately whether they have it available, and how recent it is.

Date: Tuesday, February 2, 1999

To: Keystone Aerial Surveys          FAX    (215) 464-2889

From: Karl Kehde          Phone (908) 625-0638
                          FAX    (413) 584-0238

Please send me one recent winter aerial photo on 40" x 60" paper at a scale of 1" = 100' of the area delineated on the attached Hackettstown, New Jersey quad sheet.

Please find the most recent winter photography. I assume the cost is still around $300 including shipping.

Please ship to:     Karl Kehde
                    208 Courthouse Drive
                    Morrisville, NC 27560

Please bill to:     Same

You may use the same credit card number as on past orders.

If you can, please ship the photo so that it arrives by Wednesday, February 10th.

Thanks very much for your help.

Sincerely,

Karl Kehde

2nd page faxed: Hackettstown, NJ quad sheet.

**This is a letter order for an aerial photo.** The company from which you purchase your photo may have their own order form. The phone number at Keystone is 215-677-3119. They may be able to refer you to a company in your area.

Remember to mark the exact boundaries of the photo you want on the Quad Sheet, and include the Name of the Quad Sheet in your letter. Besides size and scale, you also want to specify recent winter photography, otherwise they may send you one where the leaves on the trees block the view of roads, buildings, and other facilities. You also want to tell them you want the photo printed on paper, not on mylar. It is really quite easy. Just use the form letter above and replace the information with your own.

## Step 7: Outline the Site on the Aerial Photo

After you get the 40 x 60 inch aerial photo or map, outline the site of the proposed project on it. With the tax map or a boundary survey of the property as a guide, outline the property using yellow 1/8" plastic graphics tape. The tape is generally available in art supply stores or stationery stores.

The tape is easily removed if a correction is necessary. It is best not to write on the aerial photo because ink smudges and markers are not removable. Instead, use small post-its to identify features.

On the back of the aerial photo write the date it was taken and the scale and the property. Write on a stick-on label if possible, or directly on the back of the photo.

**Tip**

When you receive the photo it will be rolled quite tightly (2" in diameter). Unroll it and store the photo rolled very loosely (about 10" in diameter) so that it will unroll relatively flat.

When you are ready to use the photo, unroll it and reroll it on the opposite side, flatten it slightly, unroll it again, and it will lay quite flat.

## Step 8: Create a Transparent Overlay for your Photo or Map that Shows the Topography (Slopes)

If there are steep slopes on the site, you can locate them precisely by overlaying the aerial photo with a transparency that shows the contour lines.

Get the topographic map from the developer, town, or use the USGS quad sheet. Enlarge or reduce the topographic map until the dimensions of the site match those on the aerial photo. Then make transparencies of the topographic map and position them on your aerial photo.

**Tip**

When the contour lines are close together, the land is steep. Look for a stream or river or read the numbers on the contour lines to determine the direction of the slope.

*Aerial Photo*

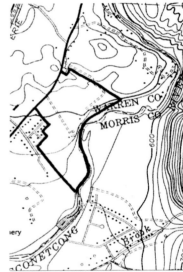

*Topographic Map*

## Working with a Map Instead of an Aerial Photo

If an aerial photo is not available, you can still succeed with collaborative planning. A map that includes the neighborhood around the project site, at the correct scale for the model buildings and recreation facilities, will work. The town engineering department or the sewer, water, or utilities department may have the most detailed map. They sometimes have maps that show exact building locations. If you can't get a map that shows buildings, try to get one that shows lot lines so you can draw the existing building in the middle of each lot. Zoning maps from the planning department will show lot lines. After you get the map that shows the most neighborhood detail, make a copy that is the correct scale and outline the site on it in accordance with the previous instructions for the Aerial Photo. Those instructions will tell you which scale to use for your size project so that the map of the entire "donut" is about 3' x 5', which is the right size for modeling the project. The correct scale will be either 1" = 30', or 1" = 50', or 1" = 100'.

Get a map of the neighborhood that shows lot lines, if not buildings.

## Scale Model Buildings

Once the interested parties gather around the aerial photo or map of the site and neighborhood, they can model their ideas for the project directly on the photo or map. We have tried sugar cubes, Monopoly houses, and M&M's, but none of them were the right scale. So, scale model buildings printed on paper are included in the Appendix. You may copy as many buildings as you want on heavy weight paper and then cut them out to use with your map or aerial photo.

Cutouts for scale model buildings are included in the Appendix.

"We're really moving streets around and moving buildings around. We have little model buildings that are to the scale of the map that we're working on, and we're pushing them here and there and talking about what we like about this configuration and what we like about that configuration."

*Ruth Smith,*
*collaborative planning team,*
*Mendham, NJ*

Five types of commercial and residential buildings are provided in the cutouts in the Appendix. They make it easier to model different kinds of projects with appealing diversity and character. They are provided in different scales so that projects as small as two acres and as large as 100 acres can be modeled on a 40 x 60 inch aerial photo or map. The standard scales used for land development plans are 1" = 30', 1" = 50', and 1" = 100'. The scale used depends upon the size of the project. Cutouts of each of the five building types are provided in each of the three scales in the Appendix.

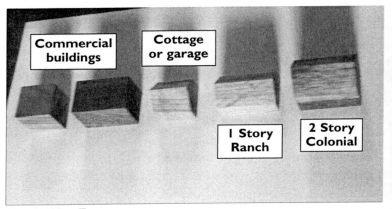

*Five Building Types*

## The Collaborative Planning Kit

The collaborative planning process is an elegant community-building process and deserves the best tools.

The need for a convenient carrying case for the little wood houses, the other modeling materials, the guidebook, and CD led to creation of the Collaborative Planning Kit. The Kit is designed to be used on project after project. Containing close to 150 model buildings and forty-five recreational facility transparencies at all three scales, it will work for projects of all sizes and types. The Kit is available from the address at the end of this chapter and from the www.landuse.org website.

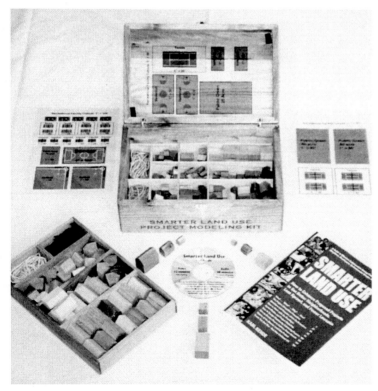

*The Collaborative Planning Kit*

*"Three-dimensional buildings have real appeal in modeling, so I decided to try making scale model buildings on a table saw. Cabinet makers gave me their scrap, and beautiful little mahogany, cherry, walnut, and maple buildings began to roll off my saw. Actually, they had a tendency to fly off my saw. Somehow I kept all my fingers. Being made of hardwood, they are fun to handle and they don't blow away when someone sneezes. They do float — at one outdoor display a thunder storm came up suddenly and they all floated to the middle of the aerial photo creating a startling increase in density!"*
**Karl Kehde, Researcher, Author of *Collaborative Land Use Planning***

## Walkways and Roads

Use colored yarn to model walkways and roads.

Walkways that directly connect key destinations are important community-enhancing features. After trying construction paper, matches, and toothpicks, we discovered that yarn works best. With tan yarn for walkways, black for roads, blue for streams and ponds, and green to encircle natural areas, it's easy to try different concepts and keep improving them. It somehow fits to use yarn to "knit" the community together. After some testing, five twelve inch pieces and five twenty-four inch pieces of each color yarn are included in the Collaborative Planning Kit.

## Recreational Facilities

Recreational facilities bring residents of the area together and build community spirit.

Public recreational facilities bring residents of the area together and build community spirit. They should be considered for each project. Modeling their placement in the project on the aerial photo is fun. We tried construction paper for the recreational facilities, but it took time to cut them out and we never knew if they were the correct size for the photo. Baseball, softball, soccer, tennis, basketball, volleyball, and even a three quarter acre public green in each of the three scales are included in the templates in the Appendix.

Recreational Field cutouts are in the Appendix.

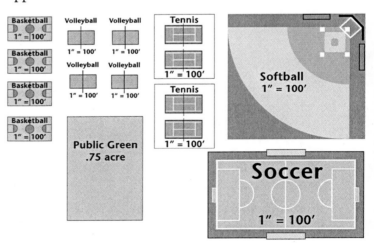

Recreational facilities that have been designed precisely in color at the correct scale are available. The ball fields are even limed! They look great, and you can actually see through them onto the aerial photo to see what would have to be leveled for their construction. A variety of recreational facilities in color in each of the three scales are included in the Collaborative Planning Kit. They can be used over and over.

## Post-Its

Writing directly on the aerial photo does not work well because the ink smudges and cannot be removed as things change. Small Post-Its are best to mark the location and identification of specific schools, workplaces, churches, post office, shopping, library, and other important places on the aerial photo and also on the map. Keep them as small as possible (one inch by one half inch) so they do not cover other buildings. Also use them to mark special historic landmarks and natural features such as the place with the best view, the oldest building, the biggest tree, the waterfall, and other significant places.

Stick Post-Its on the aerial photo to identify key places.

## Drafting Tape

One-eighth inch wide drafting tape is best for marking property lines to outline the development site on the aerial photo, or on the map if that is what you are using. This tape is generally available in stationery stores and graphic supply stores. It comes in a variety of colors. Yellow or red shows up well.

## Camera

Keep a camera with film on hand to take photos of the designs as the modeling proceeds. If possible, use a camera that prints the date and time on the photo to keep track of the evolution of the design.

"We put in a loop walking path where people could run and walk baby carriages and it's going to be scenic. I think it's going to draw the people into that area to use it. There's minimal disturbance to a lot of very pretty trees and rocks. It's going to be very nice and it's going to work."
*Audrey O'Connell, collaborative planning team, Byram, New Jersey*

## Transparent vinyl plastic

This is used to overlay the aerial photo before you model the project. Then the locations of scale model buildings, roads, parks, and recreational facilities can be outlined on the plastic with a colored marker before disassembling the model. Transparent vinyl that will work for this purpose can be purchased at a fabric store. It is sometimes used to cover tablecloths over picnic tables. Acetate or clear mylar also works well and is usually available at graphic arts supplies stores. Get three yards of plastic (makes two overlays) that is 5 millimeters thick.

## Marking Pens

Staetler Lumocolor 355 water soluble markers write well on plastic.

Marking pens are needed if a plastic overlay on the aerial photo is used to sketch the model. Use a non-permanent marker that is water soluble. Many markers that are water soluble do not write well on clear plastic. So, buy the plastic or acetate first and test the markers before you buy them. Staetler Lumocolor 355 is one water soluble marker that works very well and is available in red (buildings), green (parkland), black (roads), purple (walkways), and blue (water).

## Summary

With the few materials described in this chapter, your team has all the supplies it needs to do the modeling for your project. The next chapter tells, step-by-step, how to model a project in which community-enhancing features dominate.

# How to Design Community-Enhancing Projects

## Contents

# How to Design Community-Enhancing Projects

*People of all ages get absorbed in modeling a project that improves their neighborhood.*

*From a scar on the urban landscape...*

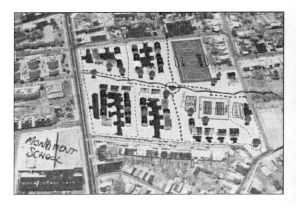

*...to community-enhancing features that brighten the area.*

### Success — Mansfield, New Jersey
**Conflict:** *Lawsuit over density.*
**Solution:** *Radburn visited and replicated in the new project. Lawsuit settled.*

In Mansfield a developer sued the town because he thought he was entitled to 400 homes in his proposed project and the town thought he was entitled to 100 homes because they had changed the regulations. The judge suggested the collaborative planning process and the developer agreed to try it for 90 days. The parties were not on good terms.

The developer, neighbors and town officials each toured Radburn — at separate times. Radburn is a 500 home neighborhood in Fairlawn, New Jersey. The homes are built on cul-de-sacs (short dead end roads), all of which border one large central park. Some cul-de-sacs have affluent homes, others duplexes, others apartments. Complete socio-economic diversity and all ages and stages of life share the Radburn neighborhood and the central park which has 7' wide paved walkways around its entire perimeter. In addition, 4' paved walkways go behind every home directly connecting it to the park. Radburn is not gated in any way and the central park is open to the public at all times. Radburn is a very safe place with an extraordinary sense of community.

All parties appreciated Radburn. They achieved some reconciliation and together reconfigured a plan similar to Radburn with 166 homes on cul-de-sacs around a central park. The lawsuit settled within six months.

*"Using collaborative planning, we settled a long standing and difficult lawsuit instituted by a developer. We visited an extraordinary development called Radburn, and then created our new project together following the Radburn concept and using this process. Instead of a mediocre compromise, the resulting concept was a model of the kind of development that we would like to have to implement our master plan. This process resolved differences we thought were irreconcilable! It is the most effective and innovative approach we have seen!"*

**Fred Wainright, Mayor**
**Ernest Beres, Planning Board Chairman**
**Mary Ellen Lister, Planning Board member**

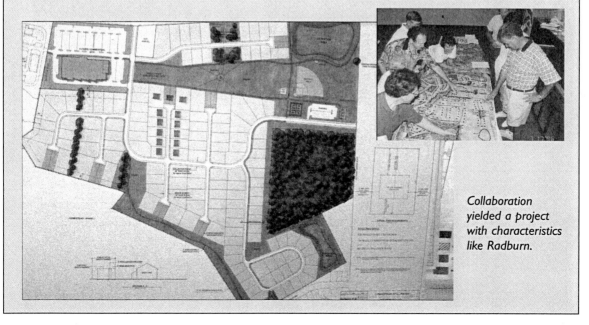

*Collaboration yielded a project with characteristics like Radburn.*

## Introduction

It's time to model the project. It's easy to design a neighborhood-enhancing project when you model it directly on an aerial photo or map which shows both the project site and the surrounding neighborhood. You can get the map or aerial photo at the correct scale, as well as the most workable modeling materials, by following the instructions in Chapter Five.

*Modeling the project directly on the aerial photo.*

## Community Spirit: The Goal of Modeling

Community-enhancing features result from team spirit among the modelers.

The goal of the modeling is to design a project that (1) knits the existing community together by adding community-enhancing features and (2) is profitable for the developer to build. The earlier chapters indicated that the proposed project can be a catalyst for building community spirit among the neighbors, and with the developer, environmentalists, and other interested parties. By working shoulder to shoulder and sharing ideas during the modeling, neighbors, developer, environmentalists, and other interested citzens get to know each other and become friends. Our research shows that when a sense of community is created among the modelers, the project will be configured in a way that builds community spirit on the ground. How? The project will evolve to include community-enhancing features such as walkways, public greens, and recreational facilities that help people enjoy the happiness and security of being with each other in community.

## The Developer, Profits, and Funding

The project that is being modeled is only an academic exercise for the modelers unless there is a developer present who is ready, willing, and able to build it. Also, it must be financially feasible for the developer to include the community-enhancing features in the plan. Projects that include friendly, welcoming features and tangible connections with the surrounding neighborhood are valuable to prospective buyers and easier to market. Sometimes features that specifically enhance community spirit and vitality will add enough to project profits to pay for themselves.

**The developer must be present during the modeling.**

*The model makes it easy for the developer to see the benefits of community-enhancing features.*

**Community-enhancing design may allow higher density and philanthropic funding.**

Good project design avoids problems normally associated with development and solves existing problems. Such good design may allow a higher density development than the local ordinances specify. If that happens, the team can request appropriate variances and the developer may be able to recover his expenses for the community-enhancing features by having additional units to sell.

Sometimes the cost of community-enhancing features can be covered by grants from state or local governmental agencies or from philanthropic institutions. Obtaining government and philanthropic funding is easier when all

"This process, which we couldn't have created for ourselves, has several advantages. First, it could be more financially beneficial; second, it has a high level of enthusiasm; third, it has an appreciation of what our community is; and fourth, I think that the group is respectful of the individual property owner's investment in his own property. So, I think it has those four things going for it."
*John deNeufville, developer, Mendham, NJ*

parties share a clear vision of what is wanted. Funding agencies like to see proposals in which the neighbors, developer, environmentalists, and planning board all agree that the community will benefit from the proposed community-enhancing features. Collaborative planning generates these kinds of proposals.

It is important that no community-enhancing feature be rejected because it seems too expensive. If the feature clearly helps the surrounding neighborhood, find the right place for it in the model, include it, and keep talking about it. A funding solution will appear when the timing is right.

> Don't reject a community-enhancing feature because it seems too expensive.

## Overview of the Modeling Procedure

After evaluating the neighborhoods surrounding the project site and listing their strengths and weaknesses, the collaborative planning team reviews the Checklist of Community-Enhancing Features in the Appendix and selects features from the checklist, and from their own intuition, that would benefit the area. With a rough idea of features to include in the project, the team is ready to begin modeling the project.

> Modeling allows collaborative visioning and upgrading of ideas.

Modeling various project concepts allows the collaborative planning team to continuously envision and upgrade their ideas. Team members configure the community-enhancing features in a pattern that fosters a sense of community among area residents. The pattern of community-enhancing features improves as the sense of community on the collaborative planning team improves.

That is why the focus on collaboration and team building among neighbors, developer, city planner, and environmentalists on the team is so important. (See Chapter Four for specific activities that achieve collaboration and team spirit on the collaborative planning team.)

The modeling itself follows a simple series of steps that include placing scale model parks, connecting pathways, buildings, and roads on the aerial photo or map of the neighborhood. Team building discussion is enhanced by the hands-on flow of ideas. The team tries different configurations of community-enhancing features, keeps improving them, and shares them with the planning board. Finally, a consensus is reached that the team has the best set of features included in a project concept that connects well with the surrounding neighborhood and is financially feasible to build. Once again, the collaborative planning team presents the model to the planning board where, this time, it is approved to be drafted into a plan that conforms with the regulations.

*Team-building discussion is enhanced by the hands-on flow of ideas.*

"Everybody has to really roll up their sleeves and sit down and dig in. This is a process to feel comfortable about sitting down and digging in. To do it you have to be more creative. You've got to bring energy, you've got to bring ideas, and you've got to be willing to be very flexible and say, 'Wow! ...hey, wait a second . . . how would this work?' "
*Audrey O'Connell,*
*collaborative planning team,*
*Byram, New Jersey*

## A Recipe for Getting Started

In the first modeling sessions you will follow a simple recipe for cooking up a community-enhancing project. It is very unlikely that your first land development concept (produced by following the recipe) will get it right. That's okay! It's just to get started.

## Modeling Step 1

Place your large map or aerial photo on a well-lit table with chairs around it. Have on hand a supply of little, colored Post-It notes, scale model buildings and recreational facilities at the same scale as your map or aerial photo, colored yarn, and a camera with film.

## Modeling Step 2

It can be helpful to place a piece of transparent acetate or mylar or vinyl over the aerial photo before you begin to model the project. Then, after the model is built, each building, walkway, road, and recreation facility can be outlined on the plastic with a colored marking pen to create a sketch of the project. The model can then be quickly rebuilt on the map or photo for future modeling sessions or for presentation to the planning board. If colored water soluble markers are used, the sketch can be cleaned up and refined somewhat for presentation between modeling sessions. Use removable masking tape to hold the plastic in place. Using a marker, draw the property line corners of the development site on the plastic so you know where to reposition it on the photo or map.

Place transparent vinyl or acetate over the aerial photo before you begin to model.

## Modeling Step 3

To help foster unity and team spirit among the modelers, follow the meeting and collaboration guidelines in Chapters Two and Four and read the Consensus Checklist around the room at the beginning of each project modeling session. Among other valuable insights, the checklist indicates that each idea contributed at the modeling session is a gift to the team from the team, rather than belonging to the individual who presents it.

*Team members' ideas are gifts to the team.*

## Modeling Step 4

Whenever anyone has an idea to contribute, encourage them to model it. Help them model it. Then, take a snapshot of their idea as modeled on the aerial photo. Take a snapshot of the final model of each meeting, as well as snapshots of other interesting models that evolve along the way. Take a snapshot of the group working on modeling the project to record everyone that is present.

Take snapshots of different ideas modeled on the aerial photo.

"Our attendance has been so good that almost all of us are always there. But, some people feel like talking about a subject more than others so the dynamics of the meeting do change depending on who is into it that day."

**Ruth Smith,
collaborative planning team,
Mendham, NJ**

## Modeling Step 5

Build a scale model of the surrounding neighborhood by placing buildings directly over the existing photographed buildings on the aerial photo. If you are working with a map, you can build the surrounding neighborhood by placing the buildings on their lots where you think they are located. If you are working with a map, do the same with the recreational facilities and walkways. Use the cutouts in the Appendix or the three-dimensional materials from the Collaborative Planning Kit. You now have a model of the surrounding neighborhood as the context for modeling the new project.

With cardboard cutouts from the Appendix or buildings from the Kit, you can build a model of the existing neighborhood right on the aerial photo.

## Modeling Step 6

Identify on the aerial photo or map any gathering places that you can find in the neighborhood surrounding the project site. See if there is a school, workplace, library, post office, church, park, shopping, cafe, etc. When you find one, mark it by name with a Post-It and also with a scale model building.

**Identify existing gathering places.**

## Modeling Step 7

Identify wetlands, steep slopes, streams, ponds, rock outcrops, large or special trees, etc., both on the site and in the surrounding neighborhood. Encircle them with green yarn or mark them with green Post-Its. These places could become parts of parks, public greens, or wildlife sanctuaries. Also note woodlands of special significance and areas with prime agricultural soils.

**Identify environmentally significant places.**

## Modeling Step 8

Mark possible walkways with tan yarn. Find two important gathering places you have identified with Post-Its and create a major walkway between them. Connect these two major gathering places together through the site with double tan yarn and call it a "pedestrian promenade." Let the walkways connecting the gathering places criss-cross the project site in relatively straight lines (higher priority than new buildings) rather than be parallel to new roads where safety, noise and air quality are concerns. Let the walkways run along the edges of streams, ponds, parks, and public greens. Review the photos of eighteen different kinds of walkways in the Appendix.

**Connect the gathering places with walkways through the project site.**

"With this process, the development concept comes up in the grass roots from the town itself. It's not an independent designer's concept, not a zoning ordinance concept, but from the town itself."
*Peter Meyer, President, Professional Planning and Engineering, Cedar Knolls, NJ*

## Modeling Step 9

Include benches along the walkways.

Although benches are generally too small to model, they are discussed here because they are a key part of planning walkways to enhance the sense of community. They provide a place for people to meet, sit, and get to know each other. Place benches along the walkways to encourage sitting and conversation. Place benches facing views, ponds, streams, and facing recreational facilities to provide seating for spectators. Plan to widen the paved walkway at the bench site so the bench becomes a paved part of the walkway. Place two benches in an L wherever many people pass by as an invitation. Be sure to mark on the plan the best locations for the benches along the walkways.

Note: Discuss benches, their importance, and who will purchase, pay for, and install them with the team and with the planning board.

## Modeling Step 10

Place a public green where the two main walkways intersect.

Place a scale model public green (from the Appendix or from the Kit) where the walkways cross that connect the four major gathering places. On the public green, place a pavilion for a band and a place to dance. Remember to follow this recipe, even if some of these structures seem like they won't work in your project. You can make improvements in the succeeding versions of the model. Keeping an open mind as you build the model is an important part of the creative process.

## Modeling Step 11

Place recreational facilities adjacent to the public green and main walkway.

Identify recreational facilities that are currently missing from the surrounding neighborhood. Place them adjacent to your major walkway (pedestrian promenade) and the public green. Place the recreational facilities together so that more people will congregate there. Also place them where they can be easily seen from roads as an invitation for passersby to participate. You will find the recreational facilities that match the scale of your map or aerial photo in the Appendix or in the Collaborative Planning Kit.

## Modeling Step 12

Place new buildings (residential/business) that will yield a profit for the developer. Use the scale model buildings that match the scale of your map or aerial photo from the Appendix or from the Collaborative Planning Kit. Place the buildings along each side of the walkways, like guardians, and spaced similarly to the spacing of the buildings in the most appealing sections of the surrounding neighborhood. Make the long side of each building face south for energy conservation. Place the buildings in groups of eight to twelve residences in diverse sizes, shapes, and heights, again similar to the character of the most appealing groupings and architecture in the adjacent neighborhood.

Place the new buildings so that their sides (or fronts) make the edges of usable outdoor spaces. Also use as edges significant environmental features and existing buildings that may be off the project site. Use the buildings to make a variety of different size outdoor spaces around existing natural features such as beautiful trees, ponds, rock outcrops, or streams. Configure buildings so that nice views from buildings or outdoor spaces are preserved or enhanced whenever possible. Connect the outdoor spaces created by the buildings with walkways along their edges and past natural features. Put roads and parking on the opposite side of the buildings from the parks, greens, and walkways.

**Place the new buildings adjacent to the walkways.**

"On some of the collaborative planning teams that I've been on, they actually go out and study the town, evaluate parts of the town that are attractive to them and bring that into the plan. What a tremendous benefit, as opposed to me, a designer, coming in and spending a few hours looking at a specific piece of land and designing it in accordance with some zoning ordinance that says this is where a street has to go."

*Peter Meyer, President,*
*Professional Planning*
*and Engineering,*
*Cedar Knolls, NJ*

*Place new buildings to form the edges of useable outdoor spaces.*

## Modeling Step 13

Place roads on the opposite side of buildings from parks and recreational facilities.

Place roads, using black yarn, so they efficiently and safely connect the buildings to the roads outside the project, and where they least disrupt community life or the natural environment. Communities with vital social activities are pedestrian oriented. Roads should be separated from the socially active areas as much as possible because they are inherently dangerous to pedestrians. Where possible, put the roads and car parking on one side of the buildings and the walkways, parks, and recreational facilities on the other side of the buildings. Since roads contribute little to enhancing the environment, economy, or community spirit, they are placed last.

## Modeling Step 14

Take a snapshot to capture good ideas.

So you don't forget good ideas, take a snapshot of the evolving model at the end of each planning session. This also insures that the developer's planner closely duplicates the model when he or she drafts the plan.

# Hints for Designing a Community-Enhancing Project

## Hint A: Keep building spirit on the team.

Experience shows that community-enhancing design comes from the heart, by sensing wholeness. Before you begin the modeling session, try this exercise to get in the right mood. Going around the room, everyone talks about a place they have been that gave them a real feeling of community or belonging. This feeling is evoked by memories of certain block parties, family or fraternity reunions, vacation situations, and other places where people have really connected. This discussion lifts the consciousness of each person and pervades the entire group with a refreshing and hearty sense of community. That feeling of community then gets expressed as they model the walkways, recreational facilities, buildings, and roads in the project.

Conversely, when people don't know each other or they distrust one another, their design for the project either won't include community-enhancing features or the project won't radiate welcoming warmth and vitality into the surrounding neighborhood. Fortunately, community-enhancement occurs by degrees. The stronger the team spirit on the modeling team, the more it is reflected in the project plan. Every little bit helps. The walkways, recreational facilities, and buildings can be easily moved about until the most community-enhancing project imaginable to the modeling team appears.

As the collaborative planning team alters the placement and spacing of buildings, walkways, benches, pavilions, and recreational facilities, they see and feel the effect on the sense of community in the project. To express a sense of community in the project plan, the group must focus on achieving it among themselves. That is why building community spirit on the planning team is so important. The more friendly the interpersonal connections, the easier it is to sense the precise project configuration that most enhances or expresses community spirit. As community spirit increases among the modelers, they model a better and better project. (See Chapter Four for ways to build team spirit.)

> The stronger the team spirit on the modeling team, the more it is reflected in the project plan.

> "You build in community because it's a contradiction. If it was very simple, you wouldn't be having a meeting. We wouldn't all be here. We wouldn't have conflicting ideas. And with this process, people feel okay about talking about those conflicting ideas."
> **Audrey O'Connell, collaborative planning team team, Byram, New Jersey**

## Hint B: Keep upgrading the model

Creatively play with the locations of walkways, recreational facilities, and the spacing of buildings. By using scale models, the collaborative planning team can easily move them about to envision alternate designs that integrate beneficially with the existing neighborhood. Keep trying new designs until the most appealing model is created or the modeling session is over. Then, take a snapshot of the model so it can be accurately recreated at the next modeling session or on paper. The better the team is working together, the better will be the designs.

*Keep trying new designs until the most appealing model is created.*

### Hint C: Replicate Radburn's community-enhancing features.

To achieve safety for residents and an extraordinary sense of community, consider planning diversified housing around a central park with walkways behind each house connecting to the park. Aerial photos of a remarkable development called Radburn, in Fairlawn, New Jersey, are included below. Radburn contains some 500 attached and detached homes connected to a central park with paved walkways from each home. It was designed and approved in the 1920s and built in the 1940s. I have taken planning boards, developers, and citizens groups through this project. The residents of Radburn are proud of where they live and have presented their Radburn neighborhood to the people on my tours on several occasions.

**Radburn is a project that demonstrates community spirit.**

*Radburn has a central park with paved public walkways connecting each home to it.*

Radburn is an ungated portion of the town of Fairlawn, completely open to the public. It has a public park in the center with seven foot wide paved walkways around its perimeter. All homes have four foot wide, public, paved walkways behind them leading from the main roads, churches, shopping areas, and a school directly to the central park. With public walkways quite close to each residence, Radburn is a safe place to live and has a strong sense of connectedness and community. Property values are higher in Radburn than in nearby neighborhoods that do not have the park and the public walkways behind each home. Many homes in Radburn have been owned by the same families for three or four generations.

"We have had a number of visits to the project site and we have walked around the town and talked among ourselves about what we liked, about what we saw, and what we would like to replicate. The participants like that sort of thing. They keep referring back to those times we were on the property or that time we went and walked through the town."

*Ruth Smith,*
*collaborative planning team,*
*Town Council,*
*Mendham, NJ*

In Radburn people of all ages and stages of life live together.

Radburn also enjoys full socio-economic diversity. Single family homes, duplexes, and apartment buildings all front on the same walkways and the park. Young and old, rich and poor, singles and families all live in the area and use the park together. People of all ages and stages of life live together and know each other. They feel secure, and they are secure. Whether your proposed project is large or small, residential or commercial, it can be designed to promote a sense of community in its surrounding neighborhood, also called its sphere of influence, or the "donut." Radburn is an excellent demonstration of this.

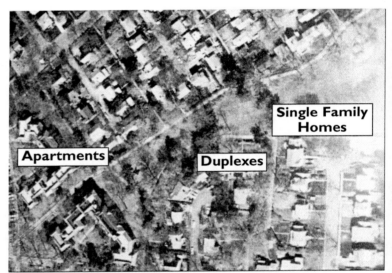

*Radburn is home to young and old, rich and poor, singles and families living in community around the same park.*

## Hint D: Put a public green and walkways in a shopping center.

Plan a retail or commercial center to include a public green and walkways connecting to the surrounding neighborhoods. When designing commercial or retail areas, consider making the heart of the project a public green with a sitting or recreational area, rather than a parking lot. The parking lots can be just as close to the buildings, but on the other side. Connect the public green to adjacent neighborhoods with pedestrian paths or bikeways so that people who live near the commercial area can easily walk or bike there rather than always having to drive.

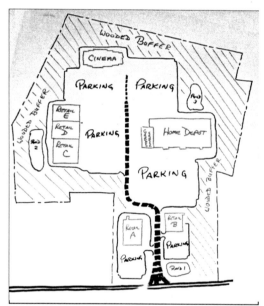

*Conventional retail center with parking at the heart.*

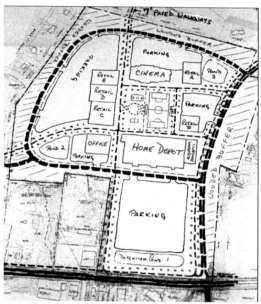

*Public green at the heart and connecting walkways and excellent parking.*

> "The people I've been working with are positive about their community, and look for ways to have the community be together rather than be polarized. They look at a design that brings people together."
>
> **Peter Meyer, President, Professional Planning and Engineering, Cedar Knolls, NJ**

## Hint E: Put alleys in the plan.

To reduce the visual impact of cars, driveways, and garages on quiet neighborhood streets, consider alleys running past the rear of each lot and short driveways off the alley to individual garages, instead of individual driveways off the street to garages next to each home. This design beautifies the streetscape by connecting all the front yards and eliminating cars and garages facing the street. Sidewalks and large canopy trees complete the picture. Visitors park on the street and walk up to front doors on landscaped walks.

## Hint F: Save the best trees.

Make centerpieces of the biggest and most beautiful trees on the development site. The collaborative planning team can tour the development site, inventorying and locating the biggest and most beautiful trees. They tie a ribbon around the tree with a number on it, and note the approximate location of the tree on a map of the site, along with the approximate height, breadth, and species. The developer's surveyor then puts the exact location of the tree on the map and on the aerial photo where the planning team then uses the tree as a centerpiece in a public green or for one of the outdoor spaces created by the buildings.

Identify the best trees on the site and locate them on the map to become centerpieces in the project.

*Marking the best trees.*

### Hint G: Make a diversified group of buildings.

Create a diversified group of homes or commercial buildings to foster a sense of community. Buildings can differ significantly in size, so use a major building as a focal point. Note the variety of appealing outdoor spaces created by the buildings. In the sketch, see how one larger building is the focal point of the little community.

*This sketch is a cluster of 12 residences on less than four acres. See how the buildings form the edges of several usable spaces.*

See how one larger building is the focal point of the little community.

### Hint H: Place buildings as the sides of useable outdoor rooms.

Rather than centering each home on its lot, consider placing the buildings closer together as usable outdoor spaces. Then, set aside the remaining land as permanent open space. The residential neighborhood will have more character, sense of community, and permanent parkland. Although individual lot sizes will be smaller, home values will be higher due to the character, amenities, and parkland. In the illustration on the next page, a map of nine traditional lots has been overlaid with twelve attractively grouped residences that use less than half the tract. Note the usable outdoor rooms that they create.

"We came up with a really good plan. It incorporates the particular traffic needs of both sides, and also the general neighborhood needs. We put in a lot of walking paths and a lot of green space. It's going to enhance the whole community. It's going to be a really pretty development and it's going to work!"
*Audrey O'Connell, collaborative planning team, Byram, New Jersey*

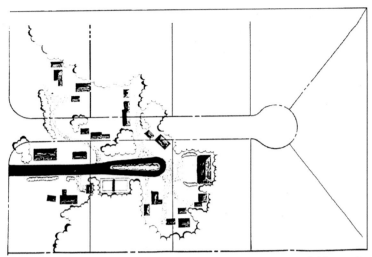

*When the twelve homes on the previous page are overlaid on nine one-acre lots, you get smarter land use: community vitality and land conservation.*

## Summary

Stay open.
One little idea from anyone at any time can profoundly improve the project.

Don't settle on the model too soon. It keeps getting better! Some collaborative planning teams have regretted that they settled too soon on their plan. Keep working on improving the relationships between the people on the team and watch the model improve. Stay open to new ideas that can come up between modeling sessions. Encourage people to take their own turn at modeling different ideas. In this work, one little idea from anyone can have a profoundly beneficial effect on the model. Invite additional people to participate in the planning and modeling. It is usually never too late to add a better idea to the plan. Changes are easily approved because the interested parties are working as a team.

Don't let old habits and strict compliance with ordinances constrict your community-enhancing intuition.

The configuration of community-enhancing features that results from modeling comes from the heart of the collaborative planning team. The spacing between the walkways, buildings, recreational facilities, public greens, and the surrounding neighborhood seems to express community spirit rather than just compliance with ordinance requirements. It is important to make sure that the configuration and spacing in your model is accurately reflected in the plan that is submitted for approval. Sometimes the people who draw the plans have strong habits from drafting conventional layouts strictly according to ordinance. That is what they usually are paid to do. Don't let old habits and strict compliance with ordinances constrict your community-enhancing intuition. Compare the snapshots of the model to the drafted plan to make sure that the plan is an accurate replication of the team's model. The team can work with the planning board about any compliance issues. Variances can usually be arranged for plans that really foster community spirit and are supported by the neighbors, developer, and environmentalists. Don't sell yourselves short.

Finally, project modeling, more than anything else, is an opportunity for the neighbors, developer, planner, and environmentalists to make friends. Those relationships are the key to building a healthy, vital community on the ground. I have seen behaviors change completely during the modeling – from cold and calculating to warm and generous, from arrogant and defensive to open and cooperative. I have seen opposing parties in lawsuits become friends and share the podium at conferences, presenting the collaborative planning process together with enthusiasm. I have seen planning boards quoted in the press as saying that the joint presentation by the developer and the neighbors was "euphoria," given their history on the project. Collaborative planning can yield "miracles" among the participants and in the design of excellent, community-enhancing projects where there had been confusion, distrust, and an unappealing proposed project.

How can a master plan support and benefit from the collaborative planning process? The next chapter answers that question.

> Collaborative planning can yield "miracles" among the participants and in the design of excellent, community-enhancing projects where there had been confusion, distrust, and an unappealing proposed project.

> "You know that you're going to be working for your own good because you have your own vested interest, and the good of the community, and you know that there have been successes in the past. So, it makes it worth it. And, like any challenge, you roll up your sleeves and get going."
> *Audrey O'Connell,*
> *collaborative planning team,*
> *Environmental Commission,*
> *Byram, New Jersey*

## CHAPTER SEVEN

# The Master Plan and Collaborative Planning

## Contents

# The Master Plan and Collaborative Planning

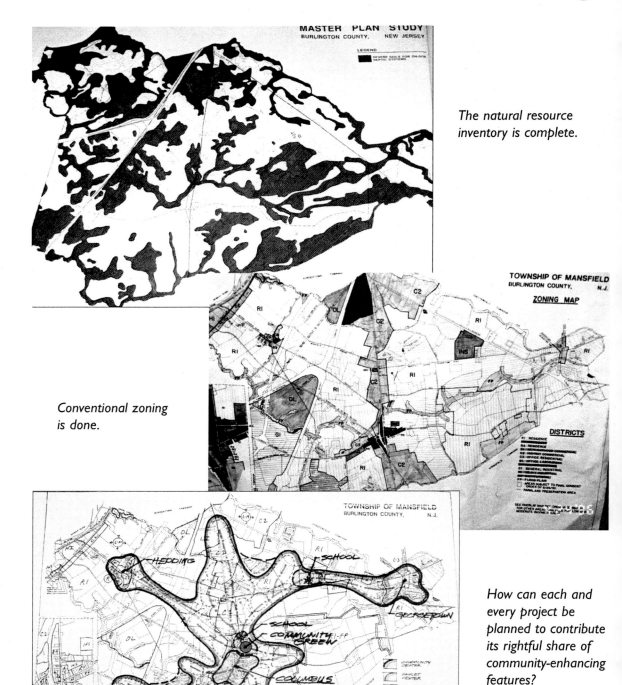

*The natural resource inventory is complete.*

*Conventional zoning is done.*

*How can each and every project be planned to contribute its rightful share of community-enhancing features?*

## Success — Blairstown, New Jersey
**Conflict: Residents vs. officials over village revitalization.**
**Solution: Relations improved. State Dept. of Transportation to the rescue.**
**Master plan for revitalization.**

In the village of Blairstown a loopwalk was created that connected a well-traveled bike/walking trail on an old railroad bed to the shops in the village, past historic structures, over a river and past a waterfall, and across a state highway. Since they were planning to widen the highway, the State Dept. of Transportation was invited to participate in the modeling sessions. When they saw the collaboration and the vision, they contributed design and financial support for improving existing sidewalks, traffic calming at the state highway crossing, and entry kiosks to identify the historic village to highway travellers.

"We, the Main Street and Village Association, a small group of village residents and business owners, had been trying to work with regular road maps to create a vision plan. We had no particular idea of exactly what was where. Several studies had been done previously that had gone nowhere.

Once we started using this process we came up with a specific direction, and we were able to prioritize the various steps. With the aerial photo we realized that we could create a loop walk that would tie the park and the downtown together, and we could see where to plan the loop. By working in a round table, collaborative group, new ideas and discussions came about regarding buildings, businesses and the value of the loop to pedestrians.

When we went to the Township Committee with our ideas, we took our aerial photo and stood it upright. We could make concrete statements since we had done the planning three-dimensionally placing the buildings and the park areas and color coding the entire concept. In 25 minutes, they were able to clearly understand our months of thought process. It was extremely positive. From that presentation we have gained decided municipal cooperation in each direction the project has taken. We invited town officials to join in. They are a part of the whole process now, and they are as excited as we are in terms of our plan development. We have now received several grants to carry out our vision of connecting walk-ways, bikeways, and parks in the village, and we have several more grant opportunities. Things moved forward with this process where they hadn't moved forward at all with alternative processes."

**Gerry Manger, Village and**
**Main Street Association and Realtor**

"People in the community were interested in this process enough to come out, and really felt good about the vision plan we came up with. This process allows the planning board and council to know what the community wants. Then, they can take that vision and go forward. It's the community's vision, not their vision!"
**Kara Quick, Village and Main Street Association**

The village of Blairstown, New Jersey.

*Life gets easier for the planning board and the master plan committee with collaborative planning!*

# What Is the Connection Between Master Planning and Collaborative Planning

| The master plan committee can encourage use of collaborative planning. |  | Collaborative planning can help update and implement the master plan. |
|---|---|---|

I am often asked what the connection is between the Master Plan and collaborative planning. It is a very positive connection. They can help each other! The basics of this mutual support are summarized on the next two pages, and the details are provided in the rest of the chapter. The coordination of the master plan and collaborative planning offers much promise, little cost, and little risk. Try it and e-mail your results and any questions to me at karl@landuse.org.

## How Can Collaborative Planning Help Implement the Master Plan?

1. By generating projects that expressly improve existing neighborhoods so residents prefer to live in the developed areas of the municipality.

2. By including community-enhancing features in each proposed project.

3. By finding community residents who are interested in land use planning, and training them in community-enhancing features, creative thinking, and consensus building.

4. By decreasing the animosity and lawsuits associated with land development and thereby giving community officials more time, energy, and resources to plan townwide community-enhancing features.

5. By increasing townwide stakeholder support for the master plan and its community-enhancing features and thereby helping the municipality attract state, federal, and philanthropic funding needed to build the townwide features.

6. By providing a collaborative model for updating the Master Plan.

7. By including the collaborative planning process in the Master Plan as the implementation component.

## How Can the Master Plan Committee Encourage Use of Collaborative Planning?

1.  By suggesting to municipal officials that they encourage use of collaborative planning with proposed projects in existing neighborhoods.

2.  By recommending that the planning board and governing body adopt the Collaborative Planning guidelines in the Appendix.

3.  By applying the principles of inclusive team-building, outward focus, enhancement, and sustainability when they update the master plan.

4.  By informing collaborative planning teams of proposed townwide community-enhancing features in the master plan.

## Making the Connection

The link between collaborative planning and master planning hasn't always been clear.

For years, whenever I give a presentation about collaborative planning, I always get questions about how what I have learned applies to the master plan. When I began this research I spent a lot of time exploring ways to make master plans better and ways to implement them. It was very frustrating. Nothing was working.

Finally, a breakthrough came when I realized that the physical structure of a healthy, vital community had to emphasize features that create community spirit among its residents. It is the feeling of connectedness among the residents that achieves safety, security, pleasing character, and neighborhood pride and identity. Walkways, recreational facilities, schools, libraries, post offices, workplaces, and other community features need to be located where they expressly foster a feeling of connectedness and achieve a sense of community. That was not happening in development projects, and I wanted to know why.

In meeting after meeting, at planning boards and with neighborhood groups, developers, and environmental groups, people battled it out over density, buffers, and setbacks. Community-enhancing features couldn't have been further from their minds. When I mentioned pedestrian promenades and public greens, they just stared at me and then went back to arguing about density. Was something missing?

The missing ingredient that would enable participants to talk about community-enhancing features was collaboration. The participants needed to take off their hats, set aside their agendas, and work as a team – a team with the common goal of building a better community. Since community spirit seemed to deteriorate a little with each battle over a proposed project, I began to concentrate at the project level. I searched for ways to build community spirit

> The physical structure of a community needs to foster community spirit. Unfortunately, discussion is usually centered on density, buffers, and setbacks.

> My research shows the missing ingredient is collaboration – and collaboration works at the project level.

and teamwork. The successes that resulted from that experimentation are great, and the previous chapters show you how to reproduce those results. But what about the master plan? In my mind I put the master plan idea on the back burner while I concentrated at the project level.

Ironically, as the master plan was de-emphasized in the research, the efforts at the project level did more to implement the goals and values of the master plans than master plan hearings and land development regulations ever did. Collaborative teams started achieving useful pedestrian walkways, centrally located public greens, efficient traffic circulation, and identifiable and pleasing character in the projects they were designing. For me the master plan had become a legal necessity that was irrelevant to getting real improvements in neighborhoods. And yet, the questions about how this work applies to master plans kept coming up at every presentation. I couldn't just forget about master plans, and that is a good thing, because I was wrong. Master plans play an important role in making better neighborhoods and improving our quality of life. After many many conversations with talented, committed public servants involved with master planning, it is clear how to connect collaborative planning with master planning.

> Master plans can play an important role in improving existing neighborhoods.

> "They had been battling for almost two years and there were three distinct groups in the battle at that point, the developer, two sets of neighbors, and the planning board. When we got called in, everybody was pretty frustrated. No one was really talking to each other and knowing what to do."
> *Audrey O'Connell,*
> *Environmental Commission,*
> *Byram, New Jersey*

## How Can Collaborative Planning Help Implement the Master Plan?

1.  *By generating projects that expressly improve existing neighborhoods so residents prefer to live in the developed areas of the municipality.*

    Collaborative planning provides a way to design infill and redevelopment projects in developed areas that, in spite of adding more people to the neighborhood, are appealing to local residents because they provide needed community-enhancing features and help solve traffic, crime, and pollution problems. This helps implement the master plan in zones slated for denser development by gaining public support for proposed projects. As residents learn that there is a process for integrating proposed projects into the existing neighborhood in a way that specifically improves their lives, rather than adding more problems, they gain interest in the neighborhood and lose incentive to move to less developed areas.

2.  *By including community-enhancing features in each proposed project.*

    Every master plan committee wants to improve life in their community, and committee members work hard to include community-enhancing features in the master plan. There are, however, many opportunities to improve community life that have not been recognized or are too small to be included specifically in the master plan. Every time a new project is proposed there is a chance to discover and build small, neighborhood-specific community improvements. With the collaborative planning process a community can seize each of these opportunities.

3. *By finding community residents who are interested in land use planning, and training them in community-enhancing features, creative thinking, and consensus building.*

Planning and zoning boards, environmental commissions, and master plan committees are largely volunteer activities. The collaborative planning process provides a way for people interested in land use issues to volunteer their time and achieve clear success with specific projects. Collaborative planning trains them to be constructive instead of obstructive, flexible instead of defensive, and optimistic about their community instead of dispirited. Enthusiastic, knowledgable citizens can turn a good master plan into reality.

4. *By decreasing the animosity and lawsuits associated with land development and thereby giving community officials more time, energy, and resources to plan townwide community-enhancing features.*

Planning board meetings relax when the developer, master plan committee, neighbors, city planners, and environmentalists together present a project plan that includes the desired community-enhancing features. Community improvement, rather than damage control, becomes the focus, and the relaxed creativity of everyone yields innovative and workable solutions for difficult problems.

5. *By increasing townwide stakeholder support for the master plan and its community-enhancing features and thereby helping the municipality attract state, federal, and philanthropic funding needed to build the townwide features.*

When the collaborative planning process is used, redevelopment projects are carefully designed by neighborhood-based collaborative planning teams who understand the benefits of the community-enhancing

"People keep telling me, 'We really intend to move into this project!' Even the other night when we went before the planning board and the town council, there were several people in the audience who came up to me and said, 'I'm going to buy one of those houses!' And I really think they meant it, because most of them have gray hair like I do and we're getting ready for retirement and you simply can't live here with a retirement income. So I think we're all looking forward to buying into this."
**Ruth Smith, Planning Board and Boro Council, Mendham, NJ**

features they include. With their enthusiasm and support, bikeways and other recreational facilities, affordable housing, and traffic calming features can gain the local public support needed to attract funding. (See the Blairstown success story on page 129.)

6. *By providing a collaborative model for updating the Master Plan.*

In a collaborative Master Plan update process (MPUP), interested residents can help the master plan committee select and plan for townwide community-enhancing features in the best locations. The use of collaboration in updating the Master Plan is outlined in the table on the next page and discussed after that.

By applying the principles and techniques of collaborative planning, the master plan committee, town officials, and the public can reach consensus on placement of townwide community-enhancing features. Then, by using the collaborative planning process with proposed projects in the areas where the townwide community-enhancing features are contemplated, the desired features can be included in the projects and the master plan implemented.

The best way to achieve community-enhancing features in the municipality is to apply the principles of inclusive team-building, outward focus and sustainability. Building team spirit on the master plan committee also helps achieve consensus, support, and funding for larger community-enhancing features. Collaborative, hands-on modeling creates a townwide vision of community-enhancing features that is easily understood and inspiring. An outward focus on including features that enhance life in the surrounding communities can make your town the heart of the area. Citizen hosting of a collaborative Master Plan update process uses the talents and energy of the public to make a positive contribution to the master plan. Citizens with successful experiences on collaborative planning teams bring their expertise to the master plan committee as members or as supportive citizens.

"This is a process whereby citizens become involved to create a positive vision, to take the traditions of their town, to take what they see in their town and create a positive vision to go forward with."

*Peter Meyer, President, Professional Planning and Engineering Corp. Cedar Knolls, NJ*

## Principles of Collaborative Planning

- Developer wants to develop the property

- **Goals:**
  (1) include community-enhancing features in the project plan
  (2) insure proposed project helps achieve the master plan

- Planning board encourages citizens to host the collaborative planning process

- Collaborative planning team includes neighbors, city planner, and participants from environmental groups, master plan committee, and the developer

- Collaborative planning team carefully places community-enhancing features on map or aerial photo of project

- Participants' focus on team-building allows resolution of difficult issues

- Collaborative planning team submits project plan for approval

- Cohesive team vision allows outside funding of features

- Trust and collaboration improves between citizens and town officials

- Shorter, more cooperative board meetings

- Enthusiasm and community spirit keeps building with each success

## Principles of the Collaborative Master Plan Update Process

- Master plan committee wants to update the master plan

- **Goals:**
  (1) include community-enhancing features in the master plan
  (2) insure proposed projects help achieve the master plan

- Planning board encourages citizens to host Master Plan Update Process

- Master Plan Update team includes citizens, city planner and participants from environmental groups, past collaborative planning teams, and the Master Plan Committee (acting as the developer)

- Master Plan Update team carefully places community-enhancing features on map or aerial photo of town

- Participants' focus on team-building allows resolution of difficult issues

- Master Plan Update team submits master plan for approval

- Cohesive team vision allows outside funding of features

- Trust and collaboration improves between citizens and town officials

- Shorter, more cooperative board meetings

- Enthusiasm and community spirit keeps building with each success

## How Can the Master Plan Committee Encourage Use of the Collaborative Planning Process?

1. *By suggesting to municipal officials that they encourage use of the collaborative planning process with proposed projects in existing neighborhoods.*

   Traffic, crime, and pollution can all be reduced as a result of using collaborative planning on proposed projects in settled areas. The public wants these problems solved, and the public becomes part of the solution as the talents and skills of local residents contribute to the collaborative planning teams. Once the master plan committee has recommended collaborative planning as a way to improve existing neighborhoods, town officials can enthusiastically suggest that neighbors, environmentalists, and developers use it.

2. *By recommending that the planning board and governing body adopt the Collaborative Planning guidelines in the Appendix.*

   The easiest way for a municipality to start using collaborative planning is to adopt the Collaborative Planning guidelines in the Appendix. These guidelines explain how collaborative planning works and how each party becomes involved so that town officials know how to encourage collaborative planning for appropriate projects.

3. *By applying the four principles of inclusive team-building, outward focus, enhancement, and sustainability when they update the master plan.*

   Consistency of values among municipal officials involved in land use decision-making is very helpful in getting community-enhancing features included in proposed projects. When the principles of collaboration, outward focus, enhancement, and sustainability are understood and applied, collaborative power can then be generated to get good projects done for the community.

"We had the opportunity, by using collaborative planning, to take a couple of major parcels and to re-establish a hamlet center there with a very attractive mixed use, mixed residential and very small scale commercial use development which combines two separate tracts and two separate developers working very closely together on one collaborative planning team."

**Ted Chase, Planning Board Chairman, Lewisboro, NY**

4. *By informing collaborative planning teams about proposed townwide community-enhancing features in the master plan.*

Members of the master plan committee know the town-wide community-enhancing features that are sought in the master plan. They know where bikeways and other additional recreational facilities are needed. They know the locations of existing conservation easements and parkland that could be enhanced by the addition of certain parcels. Their participation on collaborative planning teams brings a townwide perspective to the selection of needed community-enhancing features, and provides encouragement and support for the teams.

## Conclusion

How do we update and implement master plans in a way that ends Sprawl? That was the challenge that initiated the Smarter Land Use Project. Research quickly showed that master planning has been constrained by existing regulations, by apathy, and by opposition at the project level.

Through years of research the Smarter Land Use Project developed the collaborative planning process to focus project design on community-enhancing features and encourage cooperation among the stakeholders. It turns out that collaborative planning does much more than that – it improves proposed projects, enhances the surrounding neighborhoods, decreases animosity and lawsuits, and relieves the pressure that creates Sprawl. The original challenge has been met, but much more can be achieved.

Collaborative planning can be coordinated with master planning to make the entire process of community-building more effective. This work is just beginning. I would be happy to share ideas and progress reports with interested readers. Write me at karl@landuse.org.

"It was a rewarding experience because I thought a lot of good ideas came across. I particularly appreciated it because it took into account the sensibilities of the property owners whose properties were involved and also their financial investment in their property, consistent with the concept of developing this village atmosphere."
*Paul Nussbaum, land owner and attorney, Hope, NJ*

## CHAPTER EIGHT

# History of the Smarter Land Use Project

## Contents

# History of the Smarter Land Use Project

| | | |
|---|---|---|
| **1988** | Regional Smart Growth Plans | → Project level Smart Growth Plans |
| **1991** | Product Focus | → Process Focus |
| **1992** | Focus Inward on the Project | → Focus Outward on the Neighborhood |
| **1995** | Developer's design | → Stakeholders' design |
| **1997** | Roles & Hats | → Citizens & Neighbors |
| **1999** | Confrontation | → Collaboration |
| **2001** | Damage Control | → Enhancement |
| **2002** | Regulations | → Guidelines |
| **2005** | Isolation | → Community |

## Success – Mendham, New Jersey
### Conflict: *Large lot zone adjacent to village zone.*
### Solution: *Relationships improved. Village zone expanded with conservation buffer. Master plan and ordinances updated.*

*In Mendham large lot zoning was changed to village zoning on a ninety acre tract adjacent to the village. Increases in density were allowed in return for setting aside 70 percent of the tract as a wildlife sanctuary and including affordable housing in the project. An old, washed out pond on the tract was rebuilt in the wildlife sanctuary and connected to the existing village and the new village annex with seven foot wide paved walkways.*

"We were, I think, eight or nine at that first meeting. Then very quickly the group grew, almost doubled in size within the next couple of meetings and that's because the people that were there thought of other people that should be there. We're really moving streets around and moving buildings around. We have little model buildings that are to the scale of the aerial photo that we're working on, and we're pushing them here and there and talking about what we like about this configuration and what we like about that configuration.

We have had a number of visits to the site and we have walked around the town and talked amongst ourselves about what we liked and what we would like to replicate. The participants like that sort of thing. They keep referring back to those times we were on the property or that time we went and walked through the town. We are creating an on-going relationship amongst ourselves and I think that propels a lot of people to keep coming, because they're enjoying it.

From my experience on the planning board and developing land use ordinances, I think it's not possible to legislate the diversity that's needed. I think there are people in every community who will see the need for a collaborative process and I do think this is the only way to do it!"

**Ruth Smith, collaborative planning team, Town Council, Planning Board**

"I've learned that it's possible to have strangers come together and meet in a creative, enthusiastic way over a long period of time to meet a common goal. I wouldn't have thought that so much enthusiasm would have been generated over this.

This process put me in touch with the people in the community, so I became more sensitized to what the community really needed and wanted out of my land. The citizens played basically two roles, one, they have contributed a lot of energy and talent and effort and hard work doing things that would have had to be done anyway, and secondly, and probably more important, the citizens provided a kind of political base for the notion of doing things differently, that I couldn't possibly have generated without their support.

I don't know so many of the people that have property bordering this property and as a result of this process I got to know quite a few of them and their honest input has been very useful to me. To have a plan that is supported by quite a large number of the citizens surrounding the property, which is our goal, is something that's almost unheard of and it takes what is usually the biggest problem in developing land and it turns it into a benefit."

**John deNeufville, land owner and developer**

## Appreciating the Donors

Since 1989, sixty-three donors have contributed more than $330,000 to the Smarter Land Use Project. Through their support, countless land development projects have been improved. The stakeholders in those projects have learned a productive process for ending confrontation and sharing their expertise. The collaborative planning process evolved and this guidebook became a reality. It is with gratitude and appreciation that these donors are listed below.

Emily Allen
Edward and Cynthia Babbott
Bruce and Gail Bott
William Bradbury
Robert Becker
Bunbury Foundation
Jean Burgdorff
Charles M. Chapin III
Chemical Bank
David Emmerling
Connolly Environmental
Sharon Delvanthal
John P. deNeufville
Geraldine R. Dodge
    Foundation
Beryl L. Doyle
Karen Evans
Robert Fisher
Genesis Farm
Gregg Frankel
Coster Gerard
Dr. Michael Giuliano
Robert Graff

Leonard Hill
Ruth Beebe Hill
Michael Huber
James L. Johnson
Donald B. Jones
Laura Kane
Helen Kehde
Lawrence Keller
Robert W. King
Kenneth Klipstein
H. J. Koehler, III
Judith Kohlbach
Koven Foundation
C. Dixon Kunzelmann
William B. Leavens III
Thomas Marrotta
Mrs. T. M. McDonnell
Julia Jean Mejia
Mrs. G. W. Merck
Peter Meyer
Dr. Barbara Mitchell
Monmouth Conservation
    Foundation

George W. Morville
New Jersey Conservation
    Foundation
New Jersey Department of
    Community Affairs
Donald Palmer
Frank Parker
PSE&G Foundation
Simeon H. Rollinson, III
Roxiticus Foundation
Marguerite Ryser
Schumann Fund for
    New Jersey
Jacob J. Smith
Paul Smith
Phyllis Smith
James Thomas
Joan Tilney
Trust for Public Land
William Turnbull
Victoria Foundation
Nicholas Villa
Alan Willemsen

## 1988 – How to Achieve Exemplary Smart Growth Projects

The Smarter Land Use Project really started when I was contracted by the New Jersey Pinelands Commission to interview developers, landowners, and town officials throughout the one million acre Pinelands area of southern New Jersey. These interviews quickly led to an important insight – most people preferred their own community's land development regulations to those of the Pinelands Plan – a plan initiated by the governor and supported by the state legislature. Why were people so opposed to a plan full of good features? What could be done to gain local trust and support for the Smart Growth features of the plan? How could communities everywhere achieve the exemplary Smart Growth projects desired by the Pinelands Plan?

> How could communities everywhere achieve the exemplary Smart Growth projects desired by the Pinelands Plan?

## 1989 – A Model Ordinance and a Collaborative Process

I discussed the situation with Candy Ashmun, Chairperson of the Association of New Jersey Environmental Commissions and a member of the Pinelands Commission. With her support, a grant was obtained from the Geraldine R. Dodge Foundation, under the auspices of the Association of New Jersey Environmental Commissions (ANJEC), to research and write a model land development ordinance that would result in environmentally-sensitive Smart Growth land development.

> Grant received from the Dodge Foundation through ANJEC to write a model land development ordinance.

In 1989 I began meeting with community groups embroiled in land development disputes. The economy was booming, and controversies between neighborhood groups, developers, environmental groups, and planning boards were interfering with the permitting of many development projects. How could controversy be reduced to allow good projects to go forward? By the end of the year, observation and trial interventions with groups in Upper Freehold, New Jersey, and Goldens Bridge, New York, revealed promising ways for the opposing sides to collaborate. In the following year improved plans were produced in the New Jersey towns of Green, Hope, Mendham, and Lambertville. They were not compromises. They were good plans that formerly

> The first towns experience the magic of collaboration.

> "And one of the other things we found is that the developers in this process have voluntarily agreed to create community-oriented facilities within their developments."
>
> **Ted Chase,**
> **Planning Board Chairman,**
> **Goldens Bridge, NY**

feuding parties agreed were good plans. The results were surprising to all. In each case, the stakeholders would achieve a certain degree of mutual respect and then everything would change. Like magic, conflict changed into creative designing. How could you make the magic reliably happen? How could you make sure that the plans created by energized groups included the best design features? What would the model ordinance look like?

**Input from Christopher Alexander**

To help with the concerns about design, in 1990 I traveled to Berkeley to study with Christopher Alexander after reading his books, *Timeless Way of Building* and *Pattern Language*. Lessons learned from Alexander had a great influence on the techniques I presented during group meetings. Alexander's ideas contributed significantly to the way collaborative planning is done as described in this book.

**How can the energy of conflict be redirected to collaboration?**

Throughout 1990, work on the model ordinance continued, and many more meetings in conflicted communities were observed and helped toward collaborative planning. More questions emerged. How could you design and approve projects that really build community? Is the conflict between neighbors, developer, planning board, and environmentalists somehow reflected in the project designs? Could the clashing, mutually-cancelling energies of conflict be efficiently redirected and combined into productive collaboration? It would take years to discover the answers to these questions.

**Energized citizens help their communities and spur the Project forward.**

Citizens in communities participating in the Smarter Land Use Project contributed countless hours of time, energy, and creativity to dealing with these questions and to helping their communities resolve specific controversial projects. Evonn Reiersen from the environmental commission in Green Township; Phyllis and Paul Smith, concerned citizens from the town of Hope; Cynthia Hill from the Monmouth County Planning Department; Peter Meyer, a civil engineer from Morris Plains; Ted Chase from Goldens Bridge; and Ruth Smith and John deNeufville from Mendham were a few of the many people who helped keep the Smarter Land Use Project moving forward with their ideas.

The first version of the model ordinance was completed and a booklet on collaborative planning was produced in November 1990. Both were published and distributed by ANJEC to communities throughout New Jersey. Before the Dodge grant ran out at the end of 1990, several communities clamored for it to be renewed so that they could continue working on the Project.

The original booklet on collaborative planning produced in 1990 did not work effectively in teaching communities to find the magic on their own. The first version of the model Smart Growth ordinance did not catch on either. It may have worked if adopted, but it was dependent on zoning changes to encourage use of collaborative planning between neighbors and developers and that was a step that no town that saw the model ordinance was willing to take. Clearly, more work was needed on both the ordinance and the book.

## 1992 – Focus the Development on the Surrounding Neighborhood

The results from the first two years of the Smarter Land Use Project were too promising to abandon. In early 1992, I set up a non-profit organization, LUFNET (Land Use Forum Network, Inc.), to seek funding to continue the Smarter Land Use research. Fundraising was a challenge because LUFNET was a small, new organization, the economy was in recession, and the idea of collaboration in land development was seen by many funders as either a compromise or as off-target. Fortunately, LUFNET received a matching grant from the New Jersey Department of Community Affairs. Several family foundations, including Chapin, deNeufville, Gerard, Graf, Huber, Leavens, Marotta, and Turnbull provided the matches, as well as continuing support. Additional funding over the years came from the Victoria Foundation, the Schumann Foundation, and more than twenty other family foundations.

> The first model ordinance and a collaborative planning booklet are published by ANJEC.

> Regulated collaboration was not the answer.

> LUFNET, a non-profit, is founded in 1992 to accept contributions and grants for the Smarter Land Use Project.

> "When we started this process, we were involved in a difficult situation from the standpoint of relationships between certain neighborhood, developers and the planning board. There were very different views of how some properties ought to be developed."
>
> **Ted Chase, Planning Board Chairman, Town Council, Goldens Bridge, NY**

Research continued in hundreds of meetings with neighbors, developers, and environmentalists concerned about specific projects.

Research continued with hundreds of meetings with neighborhood groups, developers, and environmentalists concerned with specific projects, but progress was slow. Some people worried that the Smarter Land Use Project favored one side or another. Many layers of mistrust and fear interfered with collaboration. In the conflicted communities neighbors, environmentalists, and planning boards were always complaining about developers' plans, and many times their complaining didn't seem to improve the projects. Developers felt blocked in their efforts to legally use their property. Large amounts of energy were being invested and wasted as neighbors, developers, planning boards, and environmental groups became more polarized. The land development design and approval process was becoming litigious. How could the stakeholders see the community-building benefits of working together? What sort of process would enable them to make friends? A change in focus was needed to redirect the clashing energy of the stakeholders. The answer was to focus stakeholder energy on designing the project to enhance its surrounding neighborhood. Everybody could win.

The answer was to focus stakeholder energy on designing the project to enhance its surrounding neighborhood. Everybody could win.

### 1994 – Land Development Collaboration as a Do-It-Yourself Process

How to achieve collaboration without an outside facilitator?

Twin goals emerged: (1) learning how to get neighbors, developer, and environmentalists to the level of collaboration that would achieve community-building project design and (2) finding a way to teach them to get there without my physical presence. Slowly the answers were revealed. Many successful techniques and tips were discovered. Communities were enjoying success with the process. The collaborative planning process began to evolve toward its current form.

An idea: Model the project collaboratively on an aerial photo of the neighborhood.

A new, but fundamental technique was discovered. The idea of the interested parties working together to model the project directly on an aerial photo that included the surrounding neighborhood came up first in 1989. The technique showed great potential for turning conflict into collaboration. It made the existing neighborhood stand out in recognizable detail and gave the neighbors confidence in their contribution to the project design process. By including the neighborhood "donut" around the project site, the aerial photo redirected the design focus and lifted the neighbors to their correct position as host for the collaborative planning process. But, who would coach the collaborative planning team?

## 1995 – The Guidebook and the Kit

By 1995 a website (www.landuse.org) was registered to hold and make available the findings of the Smarter Land Use Project. At a meeting in Nanuet, New York, Jake Lynn, a neighborhood group leader, carried in a large stack of papers – a complete printout of the landuse.org website. That led to the first draft of a useful, stand-on-its-own book to teach reconciliation and collaboration in land development. After a number of revisions, several hundred copies were printed and distributed. Communities continued to have success with the aerial photos and modeling tools.

A Kit for the modeling tools, guidebook, and other instructional materials was in its prototype phase, and the guidebook became the rookie coach for the collaborative planning teams. I began to receive invitations to speak about collaborative land use planning as a way to achieve Smart Growth. During this part of the project, regular monthly contributions from H. J. (Kip) Koehler, as well as support from John deNeufville and Phyllis and Paul Smith, propelled the Smarter Land Use Project forward.

## 1997 – Separating the Role from the Person

A big breakthrough came in 1997. The National Park Service contracted with me to help resolve a land use dispute on Cumberland Island in Georgia. The island residents were upset with the environmental groups, who wanted much of the island set aside as a wilderness area. The National Park Service was caught in the middle. In this case, the participants generated many extraordinary ideas. The participants included island residents, members of the Sierra Club, members of the Wilderness Society, and representatives of the National Park Service. Not only did a collaborative process quickly evolve from a litigious one, but this group also came up with amazingly effective

> landuse.org, the guidebook, and public speaking begin to spread the word.

> Cumberland Island residents add ideas for removing the "masks."

> "I think the town council sees the collaborative planning process as a vehicle for providing or allowing housing that is both lesser priced and higher priced, mixed together in the same neighborhood. They clearly understand that it can be economically viable under certain circumstances and they see collaborative planning as the vehicle for allowing that."
>
> **Ruth Smith, Planning Board and Town Council, Mendham, NJ**

techniques for breaking down barriers between people in conflict. Group exercises were used to help participants identify their "masks" or "hats" – stereotypical roles that we assign to ourselves and others that limit our ability to work together. Techniques were discovered that helped participants remove the masks and hats. With these techniques, the transition from conflict to cooperation was swift and complete. It was a turning point in the research.

Through the years, in meetings with stakeholder groups concerned with forty-eight development projects in five states, certain essential truths became clear:

**Teamwork in land use decisions improves the resulting physical structure.**

- Teamwork among the interested parties improves their decisions about the physical structure of the community. Thus, building community spirit among the stakeholders is an important step in the land development design and approval process – much more important than building a case to win in court.

**Perceived adversaries can quickly learn to share expertise.**

- Once developers, neighbors, city planners, and environmentalists realize they care equally about their community, they quickly learn to share their expertise as one team, even if they have previously seen each other as adversaries.

**Simple techniques achieve the magic of collaboration.**

- Surprisingly simple techniques can be used to help people set aside the old emotional baggage that interferes with the magic of collaboration.

**People at planning board meetings become new friends.**

- Written meeting agendas, team-building techniques, and project modeling tools make it easier to recruit and maintain participation in the collaborative planning process, and make it fun to make new friends of the people you otherwise would only see at planning board meetings.

**Collaborative planning is a do-it-yourself process.**

- Collaborative planning is a do-it-yourself process. Designing a land development project is a great opportunity to build relationships since it is difficult to do good land development design without good relationships. An outside expert can't make people get along. The challenge is to show them how to get along. So, give them some instructions and tools and let them do it. They will either learn to get along or they won't.

## 1998 – The First Do-It-Yourself Collaborative Successes

In 1998 collaborative successes without my presence were first achieved in Byram, NJ. Problem projects were reconfigured by neighbors and the developer using an earlier version of this book. Many citizens of Byram donated their time and energy to the Smarter Land Use Project over the years. Margaret McGarrity, chairperson of the environmental commission, and Donna Griff, who has since been elected to the Township Committee, were instrumental in the town receiving a $5,000 state grant in 2000 to establish collaborative planning throughout the town. Visit www.byramtwp.org to see Byram's remarkable commitment to collaborative land planning.

> A grant to establish townwide use of the collaborative planning process

## 1999 – Reconciliation before Collaboration

In 1999 my son, Brendan Kehde, joined the Smarter Land Use Project. Brendan brought enormous energy, creative insight, and entrepreneurial skills to the effort. He helped improve the design of the Collaborative Planning Kit, reorganized the guidebook, and went to work marketing the tools and the techniques. His efforts to make the Project self-sustaining by selling books, kits, and workshops did not succeed because the Smarter Land Use Project was trying to market reconciliation tools to people who didn't know they could or should work together.

> Big improvements in the Kit and Guidebook

> Opposing stakeholders realized they would prefer collaboration and they now had a step-by-step process to follow.

The ideas disseminated by the Smarter Land Use Project continued to help communities resolve land development conflicts. I was invited to speak at Smart Growth conferences, statewide planning conferences, and county and townwide get-togethers in communities conflicted by development pressure. When a townwide audience included concerned citizens, environmentalists, town officials, and developers, they each realized that their perceived opponents would also prefer collaboration to conflict. And, they now had a step-by-step collaborative process to follow. A CD (it is included for you in an envelope on the inside of the back cover of this book) was created so that people could see how this presentation worked to bring the stakeholders together. It also became clear that the guidebook was ready for another revision so

> "The town benefits from this procedure by gaining a development or a project that fits into the history of the town, to the traditions of the town, to the nature of what the town is."
> **Peter Meyer, President, Professional Planning and Engineering Corp. Cedar Knolls, NJ**

that communities could quickly achieve effective collaboration at the project level and get on the road to Smart Growth.

## 2001 – The Collaborative Planning Process

In October 2001, I gave a presentation in Burlington, Vermont. Jim Fingar, a writer, book organizer, and editor with a great interest in the subject, happened to be in the audience. In November Jim and I began this latest revision of the book. Together, we have been able to clarify and organize the elements of land development collaboration that had been discovered in the twelve years of research. The result is a much simplified collaborative planning process and the all-new section on Master Planning. The book has been dramatically enhanced with illustrations by Mark Hughes and layout by Sue Ball.

As the book evolved, the model Smart Growth Ordinance needed to be revisited. The research showed that Smart Growth is an expression of community spirit and, like a marriage, cannot be achieved solely by regulation. Collaborative planning works when people agree to get together to build a better community. It is a voluntary process for achieving Smart Growth. Another ordinance is not required; what's needed are guidelines for local government encouragement of collaborative planning. The new Collaborative Planning guidelines in the Appendix reflect that emphasis on voluntary collaborative planning.

## 2002 – The Collaborative Planning Guidelines

The Collaborative Planning guidelines enable the planning board to encourage participation in collaborative planning by the neighbors of proposed projects and the developers. But that only happens when the planning board thinks the collaborative planning process might be helpful to a specific neighborhood and project. No one is forced to do anything and no zoning laws need to be changed. The legal structure for permitting projects remains unchanged. The new guidelines simply advise people that a tool is available to help achieve Smart Growth and to make the existing project design and approval process better and

> A simple, clear collaborative planning process emerges.

> Collaborative planning is an expression of community spirit and, like a marriage, cannot be achieved solely by regulation.

> The Collaborative Planning Guidelines in the Appendix enable use of collaborative planning on proposed projects chosen by the board.

> No changes in land use regulations!

easier. It is analogous to the electric company encouraging people to use energy-efficient appliances – a voluntary, but effective, intervention. The Smarter Land Use Project will gather reports and opinions about the Collaborative Planning Guidelines as an ongoing task.

**No zoning laws need to be changed.**

The publication of this book marks a time of change for the Smarter Land Use Project. Collaborative planning is a do-it-yourself technique with this guidebook as the coach. The modeling materials have evolved continuously over the twelve years of the Smarter Land Use Project – from Monopoly houses in Upper Freehold in 1990, to Tony Nelesson's twenty scale houses in Hope in 1993, to the hardwood buildings in the Collaborative Planning Kit in 1998, and finally to the paper cutouts in the Appendix of this book in 2002. The materials needed to succeed with collaborative planning are included in the Appendix of this book, or are available free of charge on the internet at www.landuse.org. The Smarter Land Use Project will continue to improve these materials so that they become more and more easy to use.

**The Smarter Land Use Project will continue to improve the materials.**

The current direction for the Smarter Land Use Project is to further apply to master planning what has been learned. The use of collaboration in Master Plan implementation presented in Chapter Seven is new. Many people in the planning community have expressed interest in this aspect of the Smarter Land Use Project, and much activity is expected.

## Conclusion

The question that began the Smarter Land Use Project was "How do we end Sprawl?" The Project has changed over the years, but mostly it has been an effort to find a land development design process that would yield projects that improved existing neighborhoods.

It did not take long to find out that strong emotions about land use were leading to controversy that somehow blocked good design. The questions became "Is the controversy itself reflected in Sprawl?" and "Is Smart Growth somehow a reflection of cooperation?"

Trial and error led to some very effective techniques for improving the relationships among neighbors, developers, city planners, environmentalists, and planning boards. People who had been arguing and suing each other began to work together as a team. Almost magically, the unsustainable energy of confrontation converted into creative collaboration that benefited both the project itself and the neighborhoods around it. In time, the techniques evolved to the point that the good results could be reliably reproduced in an easy, inexpensive, do-it-yourself way.

So, what about the original question – how do we end Sprawl? Based on our research, one answer is to reduce the pressure for sprawl development by designing each project in a settled area specifically to improve stakeholder relationships and the surrounding neighborhood. Collaborative planning is a viable tool for doing that. Currently, the Smarter Land Use Project is focused on applying the experience and principles of collaborative planning to master planning. The new question is "How can we include the best townwide community-enhancing features in proposed projects?" Let me know if you are ready to work on this in your town.

On a personal level, stakeholders report that it is very pleasant to work as a team with new friends who had been perceived as adversaries. Long-lasting, beneficial relationships can develop. Municipal officials, neighbors of proposed projects, city planners, environmentalists, and developers often find a sense of satisfaction about their community and a feeling of security that comes from knowing each other as members of one community-building team. I hope you have the same pleasant experience.

Best wishes for successful community building.

# Forms You Can Use

# Checklist of Community-Enhancing Feature

*See reverse for how to achieve these features in your neighborhood.*

## SOCIAL INTERACTION
### Activities for all ages and stages of life

____ Public green with benches

____ Pavilion

____ Stage for outdoor theatre and concerts

____ Place for dancing, with paved area & bandstand

____ Volleyball court

____ Picnic area

____ Place to play horseshoes

____ Adventure playground – wood, rope, grass, water

____ An outdoor place to build a fire and gather

____ Beautiful place to sit

____ High place to sit

____ Basketball court

____ Softball field

____ Soccer field

____ Tennis courts

____ Baseball field

____ Swimming pool

____ Swimming beach

____ Recreation located next to major walkways and in view of roads to encourage participation and spectators

____ Library

## ENVIRONMENT
### Enhance existing assets of project site and neighborhood

____ Important trees and stone walls

____ Historic resources

____ Pond for boating, skating, fishing, and wildlife

____ Habitat for diverse wildlife

____ Wildlife corridors to adjacent parks

____ Wilderness area – any size (not to be disturbed)

____ New building architecture in the best character of the existing neighborhood

____ New building ornamentation in the best character of the existing neighborhood

## SERVICES
### Desirable within walking distance

____ Neighborhood center – kitchen, meeting room, workshop, guest rooms

____ Corner grocery

____ Cafe or restaurant

____ Farm produce stand

____ Place for a community-supported vegetable garden

____ Daycare center

____ Affordable housing for all ages and stages of life

## TRAFFIC REDUCTION
### Volume and Congestion

____ Walkways/bikeways with benches, wide and paved, from adjacent neighbor-hoods directly through project site to:
____ School
____ Supermarket
____ Recreation fields
____ Post office
____ Workplaces
____ Retail stores
____ Church
____ Cemetery

____ Major pedestrian prome-nade between two most used area destinations, with spectator benches to view adjacent recreation activities.

____ Walkways and foot-bridges along streams and ponds

____ Bus stop

____ Cul-de-sac, dead end road

____ Bypass road

____ Service road

____ Mixed residential, com-mercial and recreational uses

____ Night-lit activities close to each other

____ _____

____ _____

____ _____

Compiled by Karl Kehde
E-mail suggested additions to
karl@landuse.org

# How to Achieve Community-Enhancing Features in Your Neighborhood

*Copy this page on the reverse side of the checklist.*

Any time there is a development proposed near where you live, there is a chance to design the project so that it enhances life in your neighborhood. This kind of design work is best done by a collaborative team that includes neighbors of the project, the developer, the city planner, and other interested citizens. Here is a small sampling of questions that could help the design:

Where could walkways/bikeways through the project be placed to best help people living on one side of the project get to the school, playground, library, parks, or shopping on the other side of the project?

Are there practical recreation facilities that could be built in the proposed project that would improve life for children and families in the surrounding neighborhood?

Is there a way that traffic congestion in the surrounding community could be reduced with a bypass road or bikeway connected through the proposed development?

Are there natural areas on the proposed development site or in the surrounding neighborhood that could be enhanced with pathways as part of the project?

Is there an appealing historic identity, character, or detail in the architecture of your neighborhood that could be reflected in the architecture of the proposed project?

Although the developer is not responsible for adding public facilities on his or her property, the facilities that improve life in your neighborhood will also usually improve the marketability of the project. In addition, philanthropic funding for neighborhood development is frequently available when the neighborhood has a clear vision of its needs and the neighbors, developer, environmentalists, and town officials are in agreement.

The list on the reverse side of this sheet is a collection of ideas that can make your current neighborhood a better place to live. Some of these ideas will be practical and helpful for your particular neighborhood. As you work through each item on the list, think about whether it would make the area surrounding and including the proposed project a better place to live by bringing people together, by providing facilities for people of all ages and stages of life, or by enhancing the environment. Check the items on the list that you think might benefit life in your neighborhood. Don't concern yourself with the expense of building them at this time.

Designing the new project can also be a catalyst for improving the neighborhood in other ways. Use the opportunity to discuss other possible neighborhood enhancements:

__Block parties          __Vacation watch
__Car-pooling            __Vegetable swap
__Litter patrol          __Traffic control
__Package receiving      __Recycling bins
__Watching children
__Child care swapping
__Flower planting
__Care of sick & aging
__Softball league
__Community spirit & pride
__Neighborhood get-togethers, etc.

Experience over the past ten years shows that neighbors, developers, city planners, and environmentalists can work together in a friendly, constructive, creative way. Projects and neighborhoods can both be enhanced through this kind of team effort. Good luck! Your participation in project design at this time can make a real and lasting difference in your neighborhood.

# Cutouts of Recreational Facilities (1" = 30')

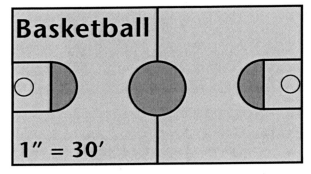

**Basketball**

1" = 30'

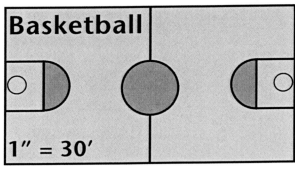

**Basketball**

1" = 30'

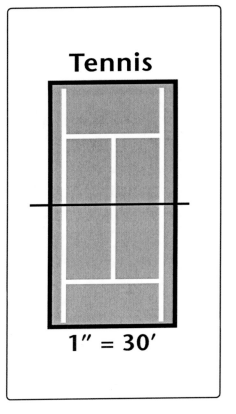

**Tennis**

1" = 30'

**Public Green**

**.25 acre**

1" = 30'

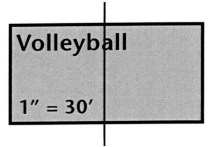

**Volleyball**

1" = 30'

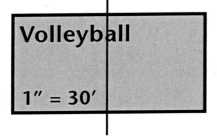

**Volleyball**

1" = 30'

# Cutouts of Recreational Facilities (1" = 50')

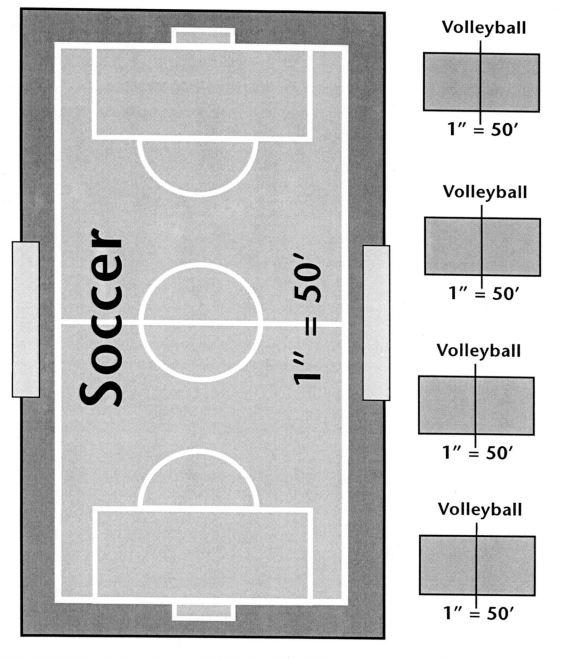

**Soccer**

1" = 50'

**Volleyball**

1" = 50'

**Volleyball**

1" = 50'

**Volleyball**

1" = 50'

**Volleyball**

1" = 50'

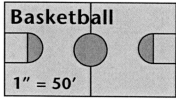

**Basketball**

1" = 50'

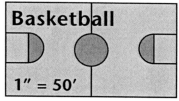

**Basketball**

1" = 50'

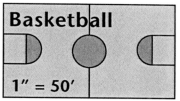

**Basketball**

1" = 50'

# Cutouts of Recreational Facilities (1" = 50')

**Public Green**

**.60 acre**

**1" = 50'**

**Public Green**

**.60 acre**

**1" = 50'**

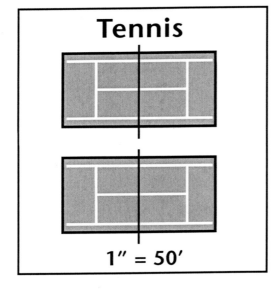

Tennis

1" = 50'

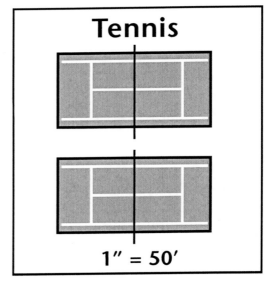

Tennis

1" = 50'

# Cutouts of Recreational Facilities (1" = 100')

Basketball 1" = 100'   Basketball 1" = 100'   Basketball 1" = 100'   Basketball 1" = 100'   Basketball 1" = 100'

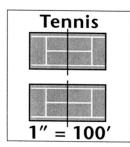
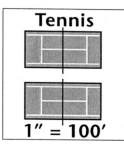
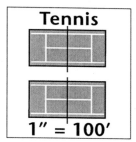
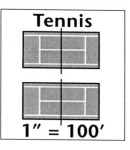

Tennis 1" = 100'   Tennis 1" = 100'   Tennis 1" = 100'   Tennis 1" = 100'

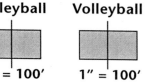
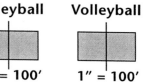
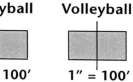

Volleyball 1" = 100'   Volleyball 1" = 100'   Volleyball 1" = 100'   Volleyball 1" = 100'   Volleyball 1" = 100'   Volleyball 1" = 100'

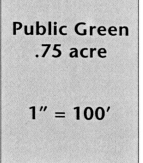

Public Green .75 acre

1" = 100'

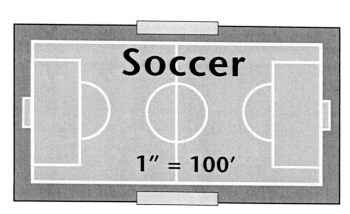

Soccer 1" = 100'

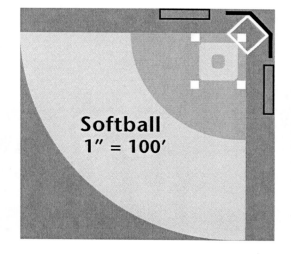

Softball 1" = 100'

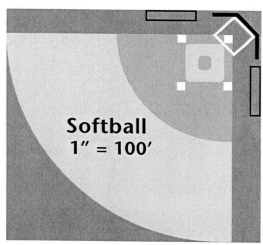

Softball 1" = 100'

# Cutouts of Buildings, Roads, and Walkways

## 1" = 100'

| Peak Roofed Residence | Cottage Garage | Flat Roofed Commercial | Office Bldg |
|---|---|---|---|

## 1" = 50'

| Peak Roofed Residence | Cottage Garage | Flat Roofed Commercial Bldg. | Office Building |
|---|---|---|---|

**Walkway/Bikeway** (tan yarn is preferable)

**Road** (black yarn is preferable)

# Cutouts of Buildings, Roads, and Walkways
## 1" = 30'

| Peak Roofed Residence | Cottage Garage | Flat Roofed Commercial Building | Flat Roofed Office Building |
|---|---|---|---|

# Consensus Checklist:
## The highest participation and creative involvement from the most people

1. We spend time establishing trusting relationships with each other. We strive for trust in one another and practice values and learn skills which foster better relationships. We realize that we absolutely benefit from each other.

2. We are willing to learn skills in team participation, facilitation, and communications.

3. We each try to be concise and relevant in what we say.

4. We may present both information and opinions. We seek to express and understand the feelings that influence the ideas we present. It is okay to discuss emotional as well as logical factors. We may express confusion, uneasiness, and intuitive doubts.

5. We do not identify with or become attached to our ideas. Ideas are a product of human interchange and rightfully belong to the whole collaborative planning team. Each person's ideas are gifts from and to the team. All issues are problems shared by the team.

6. We aim for a balance between being persuasive and being persuadable. We are each open to the influence of new information and perspectives as we try to understand other perspectives. We are open to change.

7. We each have a unique and valid perspective on the truth. We respect each other's ideas and reinforce their validity.

8. We keep encouraging quiet participants to become involved. We expect all participants to contribute and participate equally, despite differences in seniority, assertiveness, and experience.

9. We share with each other the responsibility of ensuring that all contributions are effectively voiced and heard. Everyone contributes and influences equally in decision-making.

10. We always listen for the attractive aspects of an idea. We each offer positive solutions to improve proposals, rather than pointing out weaknesses.

11. Conflict is an important element that spurs people on to clever thinking, better understanding, and greater creativity. We acknowledge the influence of cultural prejudices and seek to discuss the social attitudes that underlie the conflict.

12. We want to explore conflicting concerns to discover innovative solutions. We welcome diverse viewpoints in our design of the most community-enhancing project.

13. We consider the goal of the team above our own. We seek solutions with which we can all agree. We want to discover the choice that is most acceptable to all participants. The goal is team unity.

14. We want to be together as one friendly team.

**Consensus is a cooperative learning process through which we support each other in becoming more healthy human beings – a calm, friendly gathering to express truth.**

# Invitation to a Neighbors' Meeting

**To: All neighbors of the property outlined on the enclosed map.**

**From:** _____

_**You are cordially invited**_ to an informal meeting to discuss a project that is proposed for the property outlined on the attached map.

Meeting day: _____    and date: _____

Meeting time: _____

Meeting place: _____

For questions and directions, contact:_____

E-mail: _____    Phone: _____

    This project is an opportunity for us to improve our neighborhood. A technique that has worked in other communities is called collaborative planning. It gives neighbors a hand in designing a proposed project so that it improves the surrounding neighborhood.

    Collaborative planning involves working with the developer to find something that can be added to the project to improve it. As neighbors, we know best what facilities or features would enhance life in our neighborhood if those features could be included in the proposed project.

    Read over the attached Checklist of Community-Enhancing Features to give you some ideas. Jot down other ideas that occur to you. Then, please bring your ideas to the meeting. The first meeting will just be with people from the neighborhood so we can learn more about the collaborative planning process and decide if we want to initiate it.

    Give me a call, or send me an e-mail if you have any questions.

    Please contact me to let me know if you will be able to attend.

Sincerely,

**Attachments:**    Street map with development site outlined
                   Checklist of Community-Enhancing Features

# Sample Collaborative Planning Meeting Agenda

## Wednesday, October 23, 1998

| Item | Action | Time | Introducer |
|---|---|---|---|
| 1.  Socialize | Chit Chat | 8:00 | |
| 2.  Introductions | Report | 8:10 | Around the room |
| 3.  Personal "new and goods" (See page 69.) | Report | | Around the room |
| 4.  Consensus Guidelines (Back of Agenda) | Read | 8:25 | Around the room |
| 5.  Select timekeeper, notetaker, facilitator | Decision | 8:35 | George |
| 6.  Review last meeting | Report | 8:40 | Grace |
| 7.  Finalize this agenda | Decision | 8:45 | Peter |
| 8.  Personal "sense of community" experiences (See page 70.) | Report | 8:50 | Around the room |
| 9.  Work on project design | Decision | 9:05 | George |
| 10. Take photo of progress | Decision | 9:45 | Susan |
| 11. Evaluate this meeting | Report | 9:50 | Around the Room |
| 12. Adjourn | Decision | 10:00 | All |

# Update Letter to the Planning Board about Each Collaborative Planning Meeting

Date: _____

To:     Planning Board

From:    Collaborative Planning Team for _____ Project

Date of last collaborative planning meeting: _____

____We posted a notice of the date, time, and subject of the last meeting in a public place.

**Number of participants at the last meeting:**

   ____ neighbors       ____ developer       ____ environmentalists

   ____ planners         ____ realtors         ____ social workers

   ____ master plan committee members       ____ other_____

**Topics discussed:**

   ____ Which community-enhancing features to include in the project

   ____ How to encourage more people to participate

   ____ How to improve spirit and trust among the participants

   ____ _____

**Help requested from the Planning Board:**

   ____ Use of a copier

   ____ Space for a meeting

   ____ Encourage developer to participate

   ____ Encourage town/county planner to participate

   ____ Encourage more neighbors to participate

   ____ Encourage _____ to participate

   ____ Place us on your agenda on _____ (date) to discuss the project.

   ____ _____

**Other thoughts to share with the Planning Board:**

_____

_____

Date of next scheduled collaborative planning meeting:

_____

For further information, please contact: _____

   Phone: _____     E-mail: _____

Thank you for your support.

Sincerely,

# Planning Board Letter to Developers about the Collaborative Planning Process

The Town Council, Planning Board, and Environmental Commission strongly encourage the developer and the neighbors of each proposed project, together with other interested citizens, to participate together in a collaborative planning process. Participation is voluntary, but very beneficial to all parties. Although there are many benefits from collaborative planning, the primary purpose is to design the project so that it includes community-enhancing features that help the project, the existing neighborhood, and the larger community.

Although the planning board endorses and recommends collaborative planning and can help provide meeting space if necessary, our elected officials and board members do not attend the collaborative meetings. After reviewing a developer's conceptual plan, the planning board may suggest the collaborative planning process by letter to each neighbor within 200 feet of the proposed project. If they choose to participate, the neighbors then obtain the guidebook and modeling materials from the planning board secretary, familiarize themselves with the process, and invite the developer and other interested citizens to meet with them.

Collaborative planning may be used with residential, commercial, and industrial projects of any nature and size that have the potential to enhance adjacent neighborhoods. Collaborative planning has been shown to produce lasting friendships between neighbors, city planners, other interested citizens, and developers, and to result in better projects and better neighborhoods.

## BENEFITS TO DEVELOPERS

1. The profitability of your project will likely increase as the project is designed specifically to enhance quality of life and property values in the surrounding neighborhood and the larger community, as well as in the project itself.

2. You save money when you do your detailed planning after you have strong support for the conceptual plan. Collaborative planning usually results in efficient agreement between developer, neighbors, city planners, environmentalists, and planning board on a variety of project features. The whole approval process moves more quickly and results in a higher value project, thereby decreasing your expenses and increasing your profits.

3. You gain an opportunity to establish friendships with neighbors, environmentalists, city planners, and other interested citizens. This usually results in new ideas for improving your project and in public support for your project early in the approval process.

## WHAT SHOULD YOU DO?

Bring a conceptual plan for your proposed project to a workshop meeting with the Planning Board. After a quick review for viability and neighborhood influence, the Planning Board will then notify the neighbors. Interested developers with a conceptual plan should call the Planning Board secretary to be placed on an upcoming board meeting.

# Planning Board Letter to Neighbors about the Collaborative Planning Process

A developer has submitted a conceptual development proposal for land within 200 feet of your home.

General nature of the proposal: _____

Street address of proposed project: _____

Size of parcel(s) in acres: _____    Block and Lot of project site: _____

Developer: _____

The Town Council, Planning Board, and Environmental Commission encourage the neighbors of this proposed project to invite the developer and other interested citizens to participate together in the collaborative planning process. Collaborative planning is used with residential, commercial, and industrial projects that have the potential to enhance their adjacent neighborhoods and the larger community. Participation is voluntary but very beneficial to all parties. The purpose of collaborative planning is to design the project to include community-enhancing features and to build community spirit. This process has been used in other neighborhoods with excellent results.

This letter is being sent to the neighbors who live within 200 feet of the proposed project, but participation is not limited to them alone. All citizens who believe the project can be designed to enhance life in the community are welcome to participate.

## BENEFITS TO NEIGHBORS

1. You will help select and place community-enhancing features in and around the project.

2. You will gain the opportunity to meet other neighbors and to brainstorm with the developer in an enjoyable and productive forum. These are not boring meetings. They are exciting, creative, and positive get-togethers.

3. Project approvals become more positive and efficient, sometimes resulting in additional neighborhood improvements.

4. You will get to enjoy the community-enhancing features that you include in the project.

5. Enduring new friendships often develop.

## WHAT SHOULD YOU DO?

Contact the Planning Board secretary to obtain information about how to initiate the collaborative planning process for this project.

# The Collaborative Planning Guidelines
# for Adoption by the Planning Board

The land development Approving Authority of Anytown has determined that it is in the public interest to support collaborative planning to encourage community-enhancing features to be included in proposed projects in the settled areas of the municipality and to encourage cooperation between the stakeholders during project design.

Therefore, the land development Approving Authority of Anytown desires to adopt these voluntary Collaborative Planning guidelines pursuant to its authority to promulgate procedures and guidelines.

The objective of these guidelines is to encourage projects in or adjacent to the settled areas of the municipality to be designed expressly to include features that vitalize their surrounding neighborhoods and the larger community. Specifically, collaborative planning is expected to help make sure that proposed projects include features that enhance the existing neighborhood's sense of community, environmental health, character, housing variety, diversity of wildlife habitat, pedestrian access to municipal services, safety, traffic circulation, and property values.

## Section 1.0 – Definitions

The following words and phrases when used in these guidelines shall have these meanings:

**"Smart Growth"** shall mean land development/redevelopment in or adjacent to an already developed area that is designed specifically to benefit its adjacent human and wildlife community. Smart Growth projects build community spirit, solve existing problems, and further develop the best character and identity of the area. They also increase property values and reduce the expense of community services. They are supported by both residents and developers and are easily approved. The collaborative planning process described herein is one way to design projects that achieve Smart Growth.

**"Approving Authority"** shall mean the Anytown Planning Board, Planning Commission, or Zoning Board. The results of collaborative planning are not binding in any way on the Approving Authority and constitute recommendations only.

**"Community-Enhancing Features"** shall mean such features as public greens, walkways and bikeways, diversity in housing types, recreation facilities, wildlife sanctuaries, and others included in the list set forth in Section 6.0 of these guidelines.

**"Collaborative Planning"** means a non-binding, voluntary, collaborative process used by the neighbors of a proposed project, its developer, a city planner and other interested citizens to design a development plan that integrates the proposed project with the surrounding community by including a variety of community-enhancing features.

Through this process, these features are arranged to knit the community together, solve existing problems, provide privacy and autonomy, create the opportunity for spontaneous personal interaction in informal settings for residents of all ages and stages of life, and promote enjoyment of the full variety of wildlife communities.

**"Collaborative planning team"** means an open, inclusive, voluntary group of interested citizens residing in proximity to the subject property, the developer, and local planning staff where feasible. The objective of the collaborative planning team is to create the land development concept plan that is most beneficial to the surrounding community and economically satisfactory to the landowner/developer.

**"Approving Authority Letter to Developers about Collaborative Planning"** shall mean the letter set forth in Section 4.0 of these Guidelines, describing collaborative planning and its benefits to developers, that is given to developers when they pick up the land development regulations at the planning department.

**"Approving Authority Letter to Neighbors about Collaborative Planning"** shall mean the letter set forth in Section 5.0 of these Guidelines, describing collaborative planning and its benefits to neighbors of a proposed project, that is sent by the approving authority to neighbors living within 200 feet of a proposed project, after the approving authority has reviewed a conceptual plan submitted by the developer and found it appropriate for collaborative planning.

## Section 2.0 – Process for Encouraging Collaborative Planning

First, the developer picks up the Approving Authority Letter to Developers *(see sample in Section 4.0 of these Guidelines)* at the municipal planning office.

Second, if the developer is interested in participating in the collaborative planning process, he or she brings a concept plan to the Approving Authority.

Third, the Approving Authority reviews the developer's concept to see if the surrounding neighborhood and/or the larger community would benefit from participating in collaborative planning. If so, the approving authority sends the Approving Authority Letter to Neighbors *(see sample in Section 5.0 of these Guidelines)* to all the neighbors within 200 feet of the proposed project.

Fourth, if the neighbors are interested in participating in collaborative planning, they get the necessary materials from the Approving Authority office.

Fifth, if the neighbors decide that the project can be designed to include community-enhancing features that would improve their neighborhood, they set up the collaborative planning team and begin the process.

## Section 3.0 – The Collaborative Planning Process

When the collaborative planning team, as defined above, has organized itself to help place communilty-enhancing features into a land development concept plan for a specific property, the following steps are recommended:

(A)  The collaborative planning team should obtain an aerial photo or map, topographic surveys, and soils information of the site and the surrounding neighborhood. The town planning and engineering departments and the county planning office may be able to help provide these materials.

(B)  After gaining specific knowledge of the site and its surroundings, the collaborative planning team creates a land development concept plan that includes the community-enhancing features that benefit the existing neighborhood, the larger community, and the project itself. Information and resources to help the collaborative planning team do its work will be available from the Approving Authoriy secretary.

(C)  The developer should then draw the detailed plan that best reflects the layout of community-enhancing features created by the collaborative planning team in a form acceptable to the Approving Authority.

(D)  Presentation to the approving authority of the plan for community-enhancing features created by the collaborative planning team should be made by the team with the developer present.

(E)  The collaborative planning team should set up interim discussions with the Approving Authority to gain their input as various community-enhancing features are considered by the team.

## Section 4.0 – Letter to Developers

This is the letter from the planning board about the collaborative planning process that is given to developers when they pick up the land development ordinances that govern their project. This letter may be modified by the Approving Authority as needed.

### A LETTER TO DEVELOPERS
### ABOUT OUR COLLABORATIVE PLANNING PROCESS

The Town Council, Planning Board, and Environmental Commission strongly encourage the developer and the neighbors of each proposed project, together with other interested citizens, to participate together in the collaborative planning process. Participation is voluntary, but very beneficial to all parties. The purpose of this procedure is to design the project so that it includes community-enhancing features that help the project, the existing neighborhood, and the larger community.

Although the planning board endorses and recommends collaborative planning and can help provide meeting space if necessary, our elected officials and board members do not attend the collaborative meetings. After reviewing a developer's conceptual plan, the planning board will suggest the collaborative planning process by letter to each neighbor within 200 feet of the proposed project. If they choose to participate, the neighbors then obtain the guidebook and modeling materials from the planning board secretary, familiarize themselves with the procedure, and invite the developer and other interested citizens to meet with them.

Collaborative planning is used with residential, commercial, and industrial projects of any nature and size that have the potential to enhance adjacent neighborhoods. Collaborative planning has been shown to produce lasting friendships between neighbors, other interested citizens, and developers, and to result in better projects and better neighborhoods.

## BENEFITS TO DEVELOPERS

1.  The profitability of your project will likely increase as the project is designed specifically to enhance quality of life and property values in the surrounding neighborhood as well as in the project itself.

2.  You save money when you do your detailed planning after you have strong support for the conceptual plan. Collaborative planning usually results in efficient agreement between developer, neighbors, city planners, environmentalists, and planning board on a variety of project features. The whole approval process moves more quickly and results in a higher value project, thereby decreasing your expenses and increasing your profits.

3.  You gain an opportunity to establish friendships with neighbors, environmentalists, and other interested citizens. This usually results in new ideas for improving your project and in public support for your project early in the approval process.

## WHAT SHOULD YOU DO?

Bring a conceptual plan for your proposed project to a workshop meeting with the planning board. After a quick review for viability and neighborhood influence, the planning board will then notify the neighbors. Interested developers with a conceptual plan should call the planning board secretary to be placed on an upcoming planning board meeting agenda.

## Section 5.0 – Letter to Neighbors

This is the letter that is sent by the planning board to neighbors of a proposed project after the planning board has determined from a developer's concept that the project is located in an area that would benefit from using the collaborative planning process. This letter may be modified by the planning board as needed.

## A LETTER TO THE NEIGHBORS
## OF A PROPOSED LAND DEVELOPMENT

A developer has submitted a conceptual development proposal for land within 200 feet of your home.

General nature of the proposal: _____

Street address of proposed project: _____

Size of parcel(s) in acres:_____    Block and Lot of project site: _____

Developer: _____

The Town Council, Planning Board, and Environmental Commission encourage the neighbors of this proposed project to invite the developer and other interested citizens to participate together in the collaborative planning process. Collaborative planning is used with residential, commercial, and industrial projects that have the potential to enhance their adjacent neighborhoods and the larger community. Participation is voluntary, but very beneficial to all parties. The purpose of collaborative planning is to design the project to include community-enhancing features and to build community spirit. This process has been used in other neighborhoods with excellent results.

This letter is being sent to the neighbors who live within 200 feet of the proposed project, but participation is not limited to them alone. All citizens who believe the project can be designed to enhance life in the community are welcome to participate.

## BENEFITS TO NEIGHBORS
1.  You will help select and place community-enhancing features in and around the project.

2.  You will gain the opportunity to meet other neighbors and to brainstorm with the developer in an enjoyable and productive forum. These are not boring meetings. They are exciting, creative, positive get-togethers.

3.  Project approvals become more positive and efficient, sometimes resulting in additional neighborhood improvements.

4.  You will get to enjoy the community-enhancing features that you include in the project.

5.  Enduring new friendships often develop.

## WHAT SHOULD YOU DO?
Contact the Planning Board secretary to obtain information on participation in the collaborative planning process.

# Section 6.0 – Community-Enhancing Features

## How to include community-enhancing features in proposed development projects

Any time there is a proposed development in a settled area, a special opportunity opens up to design the project so that it enhances life in the surrounding neighborhood. This kind of design work is best done by a collaborative team that includes neighbors of the project, the developer, city planner, and other interested citizens. Here is a small sampling of questions that can be asked about the project to help with the design:

How could walkways/bikeways through the project help people living outside the project get to the school, playground, library, parks, or shopping on the opposite side of the project?

Are there practical recreational facilities that could be built in the proposed project that would improve life for children and families in the surrounding neighborhood?

Is there a way that traffic congestion could be reduced with bypass or service roads, cul-de-sacs, or bikeways/walkways as part of the proposed development?

Are there beautiful natural areas on the proposed development site or in the surrounding neighborhood that could be enhanced or accessed by pathways as part of the project?

Is there an appealing historic identity, character, or detail in the architecture in the surrounding neighborhood that could be reflected in the architecture of the proposed project?

Although the developer is not responsible for adding public, community-enhancing features on his or her property, the features that improve life in the surrounding neighborhood will also usually improve the marketability of the project. In addition, philanthropic funding for community-enhancing features is frequently available when the neighborhood has a clear vision of its needs and the neighbors, developer, environmentalists, and town officials are in agreement. The collaborative planning team may choose to pursue such philanthropic funding for the features they desire.

Some of the community-enhancing features on the following list will be practical and helpful in making the neighborhood surrounding a proposed project a better place to live. The collaborative planning team considers whether each feature would be helpful to the area by bringing people together, by providing facilities for people of all ages and stages of life, or by enhancing the environment. They check the features on the list that they think might benefit life in the neighborhood and, initially, don't concern themselves with the expense of building them. By the end of the process, the team will select the features that most enhance the community and are practically and financially feasible.

# COMMUNITY-ENHANCING FEATURES

## SOCIAL INTERACTION
### Activities for all ages and stages of life

____ Public green with benches

____ Pavilion

____ Stage for outdoor theatre and concerts

____ Place for dancing, with paved area and bandstand

____ Volleyball court

____ Picnic area

____ Place to play horseshoes

____ Adventure playground – wood, rope, grass, water

____ An outdoor place to build a fire and gather

____ Beautiful place to sit

____ High place to sit

____ Basketball court

____ Softball field

____ Soccer field

____ Tennis courts

____ Baseball field

____ Swimming pool

____ Swimming beach

____ Recreation located next to major walkways and in view of roads to encourage participation and spectators

____ Library

## ENVIRONMENT
### Enhance existing assets of project site and neighborhood

____ Important trees and stone walls

____ Historic resources

____ Pond for boating, skating, fishing, and wildlife

____ Habitat for diverse wildlife

____ Wildlife corridors to adjacent parks

____ Wilderness area – any size (not to be disturbed)

____ New building architecture in the best character of the existing neighborhood

____ New building ornamentation in the best character of the existing neighborhood

## SERVICES
### Desirable within walking distance

____ Neighborhood center – kitchen, meeting room, workshop, guest rooms

____ Corner grocery

____ Cafe or restaurant

____ Farm produce stand

____ Place for a community-supported vegetable garden

____ Daycare center

____ Affordable housing for all ages and stages of life

## TRAFFIC REDUCTION
### Volume and Congestion

____ Walkways/bikeways with benches, wide and paved, from adjacent neighbor-hoods directly through project site to:
 ____ School
 ____ Supermarket
 ____ Recreation fields
 ____ Post office
 ____ Workplaces
 ____ Retail stores
 ____ Church
 ____ Cemetery

____ Major pedestrian prome-nade between two most used area destinations, with spectator benches to view adjacent recreation activities.

____ Walkways and foot-bridges along streams and ponds

____ Bus stop

____ Cul-de-sac, dead end road

____ Bypass road

____ Service road

____ Mixed residential, commercial and recreational uses

____ Night-lit activities close to each other

____ _____

____ _____

____ _____

____ _____

____ _____

The project can also be a catalyst for improving the neighborhood in less tangible ways. The collaborative planning team can also use the opportunity to brainstorm about such enhancements as:

| | | |
|---|---|---|
| ___ Block parties | ___ Flower planting | ___ Community spirit and pride |
| ___ Car-pooling | ___ Softball league | ___ Child care swapping |
| ___ Litter patrol | ___ Vacation watch | ___ Care of sick and aging |
| ___ Watching children | ___ Vegetable swap | ___ Recycling bins |
| ___ Package receiving | ___ Traffic control | ___ Neighborhood get-togethers, etc. |

## Section 7.0 – Law

The Collaborative Planning Guidelines are non-binding on the Approving Authority and the participants. They offer a voluntary, collaborative process that can cause proposed projects in settled areas to be designed to contribute to the Smart Growth of the municipality.

---

For additional information, please contact:
Karl Kehde
Smarter Land Use Project
karl@landuse.org
(908) 625-0638

# Walkway Examples

Flagstone

Asphalt

Flagstone

Cedar bark chips

Brick in cement

Yes, it's water!

Asphalt

Brick

Leaves on dirt

# More Walkway Examples

Concrete

Cut stone

Bricks in grass

Asphalt

Cedar chips

Wood planks

Gravel

Wood planks

Grass

## About the Author

Karl Kehde was a member of New Jersey Governor Byrne's original Pinelands Review Committee to determine land use policy for one million acres of Pinelands. He also served five years on an Advisory Committee working on New Jersey's State Development Plan, and eight years as a member of his town planning board. He was a member of the Board of Directors of the American Clean Water Association and, as a developer, received a Special Award of Merit from the United States Environmental Protection Agency and was awarded the Distinguished Planning Citation by the American Planning Association.

Karl personally designed, developed, and marketed three major residential real estate projects. He has built active and passive solar homes, implemented energy and wildlife conservation deed restrictions, and donated land to conservation organizations.

For the past twelve years Karl has worked independently – being funded philanthropically – with neighborhood groups, developers, planners, and environmentalists involved in forty-eight separate proposed land developments to research the collaborative planning process detailed in this book. He has written *Collaborative Land Use Planning* and invented the Collaborative Planning Kit so that you can succeed with this process on your own with no outside assistance.

Karl has a Bachelor of Science in Mechanical Engineering and a Bachelor of Arts from Lehigh University. He also holds a Masters in Business Administration from Rutgers University. And he served three years as a lieutenant in the U.S. Marines.

*"Karl Kehde has raised our knowledge and opened possibilities that I never thought possible. His experience offers many alternatives in thinking, relating, and in land development.*

*Karl consistently reminds us that people will make the right decision if all 'hats' or 'agendas' are exposed without fear. Alleviating fear is not easy nor often addressed. It's what teddybears do for children. It's what communities are supposed to do for people. Thank you, Karl, for teaching me not to let fear run the process."*

**Carolyn R. Vadala,**
**Community leader,**
**Bloomfield, NJ**